BOBBI BROWN TEENAGE BEAUTY
EVERYTHING YOU NEED TO LOOK PRETTY, NATURAL, SEXY & AWESOME

BOBBI BROWN & ANNEMARIE IVERSON

EBURY
PRESS

TO YOUNG WOMEN EVERYWHERE WHO NEED A BOOST OF SELF-CONFIDENCE TO REALIZE HOW BEAUTIFUL AND AMAZING THEY REALLY ARE AND TO THE TEENAGE GIRLS WHO HELPED CREATE THIS BOOK. THANKS FOR SHARING YOUR INSECURITIES AND YOUR OPTIMISM.

BOBBI BROWN TEENAGE BEAUTY

CONTENTS

FOREWORD   ON BEING BROOKE BY BROOKE SHIELDS

I WAS THE GIRL WHO HAD IT ALL AS A TEEN, BUT JUST WANTED TO FEEL WELCOME AT THE SCHOOL LUNCH TABLE...

I was envisioned as the face of the '80s: The most beautiful young model in Calvin Klein's ads for his jeans; the most celebrated young actress in movies like *Blue Lagoon* and *Endless Love*. The weird thing was I didn't see myself that way. And I didn't think other kids could possibly see me that way. But that's all they talked about and all they heard.

Only when I was in that environment did I feel celebrated. And even then I was just playing the pretty girl. I'd leave school and I'd go to work. Bobbi would sometimes do my makeup; someone would do my hair. We'd do pictures. Then I'd go home to do my homework. It was a job and I assumed that everyone knew that. But the other kids thought that I was buying into that image. It was a lot of work to convince them otherwise.

All I wanted as a teenager was to be accepted by my peers. I was ostracized because I was pretty and my picture was everywhere. No one would sit with me at the lunch table. The only place I was welcome was at the teachers' table...and that made me all the more hated. I hated the nicknames, like "doll." I'd walk into the class and I'd

hear: "Here comes the Brooke doll!" Once I sat down at my desk to find a Brooke doll hanging in a noose.

I was constantly under scrutiny. If anything was wrong—like if I got a pimple—well, the assumption was I couldn't get a pimple just like everyone else. I wanted to be a cheerleader. But at 6'1", I was the tallest and I was always put at the end or at the bottom (talk about not fitting in).

My life was the antithesis of the roles I'd played. I was very unaware of my actual self as a teenager. My perception of myself was so skewed: There was one version of me in movies or in ads and then there was another me who went to school every day just like everyone else. I was focused on being accepted. I so wanted to fit in that I didn't even know who I was. The odd thing was we'd all look through the magazines and I'd be there saying: "I want to look like Cindy Crawford or Stephanie Seymour." Or, "Oh my God, I want to look like that!" I didn't for one second think I was in that category. After I did sensual, sexual roles, people made that same assumption about me. In college it was such a big deal when it came out ..."Kids...I'm still a virgin."

What happened was that everyone was so busy looking at me that I didn't regard myself. I had this avoidance: "That's not me...that's not me... that's not me." My desire for acceptance was stronger than anything. Looking back (I know it's hard to care about this when you're a teenager), I wish I'd been able to care less about fitting in and more about finding out who I really was independent of my peers. I wish I spent more time just being me. Now I get it: It's okay to try to fit in as long as you don't compromise who you are.

When I'd arrive at the studio after school I was always happy to see Bobbi because she was like the cool mom (even though she didn't have kids then) you wanted to be around. A lot of the people I worked with used a lot of makeup, and tried making me look like a different person. Bobbi didn't put on a ton of makeup. She didn't come in and want to drastically change your face. Bobbi always projected genteel warmth as if to say "we're in this together." Her approach? Figuring what was the least amount of makeup I could get away with.

Now, I'm much more aware of how much I need her. It's a bigger deal now—I'm so aware of the many different techniques that exist. And now that I'm older I've gotten more paranoid. But with Bobbi, it's still the same approach. My face is the same and she still focuses on how I can look my best. Makeup is not an easy thing to do—the way you do one person's face is not the way you'd do another's. Bobbi gets this.

People assume that any makeup will do with me. They assume that I don't have anything to worry about. But only someone like Bobbi is aware of my strengths and weaknesses. Bobbi knows how to make the most of my assets.

My message to teens (and Bobbi's, too) is to look for your own strengths. The individualism of those strengths makes you who you are. And that makes you individualistically perfect. The assumption should be that everyone is perfect. And that means **you**.

As a teen who relied on Bobbi Brown the makeup artist, I promise you're in good hands with *Bobbi Brown Teenage Beauty*. As an adult who still relies on Bobbi Brown the makeup artist **and** Bobbi Brown the friend, I guarantee that her lessons on life and makeup will take you far.

A LETTER FROM BOBBI

Hi!

I wanted to do a book for teens because I see so many beautiful girls who don't appreciate what's special about them. It's easy to find what's pretty in other people but in ourselves we tend to see only what we don't like. I'm writing the book I wish I'd had when I was a teen. For the days I felt "unpretty." For when I felt that I'd never look like the "tall blond girls." For straight answers to all my stupid beauty questions. But mostly, I wish I'd had this book so that I would have known that I was okay just the way I was, that there's more than one way to be pretty and that none of my questions would ever be considered "stupid."

Try to think of every young woman in this book as your friend—someone who's here to help you figure out those confusing things that keep you from being happier and more relaxed about your looks. The point of this book is to take the mystery out of all those confusing acts (like, How do you curl eyelashes anyhow? What do I do with shadow?) and rituals (How do I deal with my eyebrows?) that the totally together girl seems to do with her eyes closed. But the fact is that even the Patty Perfect of your life (that girl you envy deep down) probably has a few insecurities of her own.

The one thing I wish I'd known as a teen is that most women and girls suffer from a lack of self-esteem. The good news is that, with time, all of us gain a certain amount of self-acceptance. And self-acceptance to me is the key to looking pretty—if you are happy being who you are, you will look your prettiest. If there's one thing I want every girl to take from this book, it's the ability to discover and celebrate her own unique beauty.

I know the teen years are not the easiest time to "just be you" or in any way different from all the girls around you. It's natural to want to fit in—and to be accepted. But it's also important to know when fitting in means losing yourself—when conforming takes you past the point of knowing who you are. That's not healthy or positive.

We can change our hair color and even our eye color. We can improve our bodies and our skin texture. We can learn to use makeup to emphasize our eyes or downplay a feature. But self-acceptance involves learning to live with (and treasure) those fundamental things we can't change—our height, build, skin color, strong nose, pale skin, freckles, etc., the very features that make each of us beautiful and unlike anyone else. So turn the page and start picturing exactly what makes you special: together we'll turn that into your own personal beauty style.

Bobbi Brown

BOBBI SPEAK:
ONCE A TEEN...ON TEENS

It's true that I haven't been a teenager in a long time. But the feelings I experienced then were so intense—both good and bad—that I'll never forget them. I'm convinced that happiness and heartache hit you harder when you're young. The most important thing for you to remember is that everyone is going through the same highs and lows. Here are some teen moments that'll never go away for me.

Worst Moments:

- My parents' divorce.
- The time when, as a punishment for something I'd done, I wasn't allowed to go to a cooking class with my friends.
- The semester I got a D in spelling. (I pulled off an A the next term.)

Best Moments:

Hanging with my friends—line dancing with them at bar mitzvahs, creating a shop with my friends in my basement where we sold jewelry and hand-made things, seeing the Jackson 5 in concert with my friends.

Hated Most About Myself:

my big chest

Liked About Myself:

my hair and my skin

Biggest Teenage Beauty Mistakes:

- overtweezing my brows
- overdoing makeup and not realizing that I was pretty when I looked natural

Biggest Teenage Beauty Breakthrough:

realizing that with the right haircut I could let my hair dry naturally

Early Signs of Makeup Genius:

I got my first job in beauty when I was fifteen or sixteen at a small cosmetics store near my home in Chicago. Before I was able to sell makeup, I had to be trained. And the first step was learning to make myself up. (I'd already had ten to twelve years' experience watching my mother expertly do her own makeup and many years practicing on myself, my dolls, and my little brother and sister.) My favorite product? My mother's cream bronzer. It still is.

First Bad Makeover:

My own makeover began with white concealer to lighten up circles under my eyes and a pink foundation to combat my too-yellow skin tone. It was at this point in my life that I plucked and reshaped my eyebrows to look as if I'd seen a ghost. (Their natural shape was already history!) My eyes, I was told, are very small—thus, I was told, I had to learn the "tricks" to make my eyes look larger and my lids seem bigger. So white shadow went on my eyelid, dark brown into my crease with "wings" off the outer corner of my eyes to make them seem rounded. Lots of black mascara was piled on. I also remember wearing colors like copper, iced blue, and violet, but I'm not really sure why.

Then, I was to hear how my nose needed shading since the shape was not small enough. My cheeks, I was told, need shading to create cheekbones. (By the way, no sixteen-year-old is supposed to have cheekbones!) White shimmer highlighter was supposed to help bring out the cheekbones that weren't even there.

Looking back now I realize that it wasn't the makeup artist's fault. This was how makeup was taught and applied. But deep inside me I knew then that something was seriously wrong and that eventually I would find a way to make things more real and natural.

My Teen Idol:

Ali MacGraw

What I Think of Her Now:

she's still awesome and beautiful

What Teen Girls Should Avoid Altogether:

perms

trying to use makeup to contour their noses so
  they look smaller

5 Things That Irritate Me a Lot:

1. mothers who try to make their daughters insecure about their looks.

2. mothers who try to make their daughters into
the mirror image of themselves.

3. makeup that's overdone to make a girl **less**
pretty.

4. avoiding eye contact with others (it's a sad sign
that the person has a bad self image).

5. limp handshakes.

10 Things I Always Love:

  1. freckles

  2. big lips

  3. penny loafers

  4. strong noses—especially noses with bumps

  5. strong bodies

  6. cleft chins

  7. worn blue jeans

  8. anything **pink**

  9. bright toenail polish

  10. my 3 sons and hubby/best friend

Every teen girl's biggest beauty secret weapon:

her **smile**!

Something to bank on:

pimples can always be covered up

**What I want every young woman to take away
from this book:**

you can't (and shouldn't want to) change who you
are....The minute you accept what you have and
feel special for possessing those qualities, the
sooner you will really feel pretty—inside and out.

**Age When I Got Past My Self-Criticism and
Finally Started to Like Myself:**

19 or 20…and still working on it…

01 THE PRETTY MAKEUNDER
BEFORE & AFTER

My idea of the perfect makeover is to make a girl prettier, *naturally*. I like to look for a teen's special feature—her skin, lips, eyes, freckles, even her "naturalness," and use simple techniques to draw it out. The most important thing? That your make-up not be too obvious.

YOU SHOULD STAND OUT,
NOT YOUR MAKEUP!

It's always fun to look at before and after pictures. And who doesn't love to judge—searching for the after that we think is worse than the before? But you won't find anything like that here. These make-unders (I don't believe in makeovers since they tend to involve lots of makeup and a masking of who you really are) are all about making subtle changes and drawing out each girl's own natural beauty.

Before: Can't beat Sabrina's smile. After: We evened out her skintone and lightened up under her eyes with concealer. We added a pale pink blush and lip gloss.

Before: Tia is cute and comfortable with herself.

After: I evened out her skin tone, which is subtle but key. (In the "before," different areas of her face are different shades, and the cheeks "pop" since the skin tone is lighter.) We pushed her bangs to the side to show off her gorgeous face shape. And I did a rosy, natural look.

Before: Lauren's long blond hair is the focus of her look. It's crazy to overpower her natural beauty with a lot of makeup.

After: I did a quiet definition of the eye with a little smudged liner and mascara, and I toned down her shiny forehead with powder.

Before: Rebecca has beautiful skin but is a little dark under her eyes.

After: I used a little concealer under the eye, and filled in her brow to open up the eye area. I added some pink blush to the apples of her cheeks. The result? A prettier, healthier look.

2

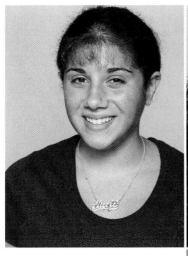

Before: Nicole has such a pretty face. Why is she trying to hide under her bangs?

After: I wanted to play up her luscious features—and let that amazing hair down! Where I focused: her eyes are now more noticeable but still very natural; her lips are full and gorgeous, so I gave them a little more emphasis.

Before: Alexandria has adorable freckles, a boyish cut, and a simple, natural style.

After: I let her freckles show through, and applied just a little shine on her eyelid and gloss on her lips. Now her natural look has a bit more polish.

Before: It's hard to find a reason to do a makeover on Nina (she's so pretty!), but if you look closely, you'll see that her complexion is uneven.

After: I evened out her skin tone with warm foundation, used banana shadow on her lids, filled in her brow, and I did one coat of blue mascara.

Before: Alyce has happy, healthy good looks. So pretty.

After: I used pink shine to open up her eyes and added slate eyeliner to her top lid. Defined the brow as a way of framing her face. The result? A more polished pretty.

Before: Jamie has a great smile.

After: Okay…so the blowout is a big part of this makeunder… But there are a few makeup lessons, too. Her skin shine is toned down with powder on a puff. To help open up her eyes, I did mascara on the outer lashes only. She is gorgeous, and boy, does she show it!

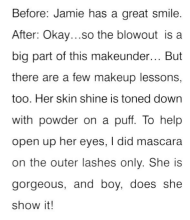

Before: Indre has a perfect oval face and a great clean look.

After: I used a tiny bit of concealer to cover redness around her eyes. Then, for a "night out look," I did a white shadow, black mascara (top lashes only), and a bright pastel pink lip color. I brushed on a bit of pink blush to add some color. She's ready to party.

Before: Gretchen's got all the makeup basics. I wanted to show her how to bring some soft color to her face...(talk about subtle!).
After: I used a little concealer under her eyes and mocha shadow on her eyelid. Then I brushed a warm plum blush over her cheeks.

Before: Haley has that natural beauty that will stay with her forever.
After: A little black mascara, white eyeshadow, and pink lips make her a knockout.

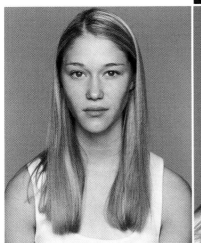 

Before: Jen has gorgeous and simple good looks.
After: Still gorgeous and simple, but now glowing. I did a soft pink shadow on her lid and filled in her brow to help define the eye area. Then I applied just a little gloss on her lips. She looks like a fairy princess…

02 BOBBI'S 10 BASIC RULES OF TEEN BEAUTY

1. Rules do apply.

Knowing what's appropriate with makeup really matters. There's a time and a place for a smudged black eye and it's *not* in your Monday-morning American history class. Save the drama for the school play or going out. Wait until high school to experiment with anything more than gloss, mascara, blush, and concealer. Whether you are thirteen or nineteen, just keep makeup simple and natural for school and everyday hanging with your friends.

2. Finger paint.

It's not cool or modern to be too perfect with make-up. (Lip brushes were created for the over-thirty crowd!) Dabbing on a lip stain with your finger is the way to go. Be loose. Spread it on. Have fun with it. Don't be too glued to the mirror. Express yourself! What's the worst thing that could happen? You'll have to blend a color to tone it down or, if you're really unhappy, wash it off and start over.

3. Skip foundation.

You don't need all-over foundation. And don't be concerned with highly technical serious makeup techniques, like contouring or shadowing. What you really can use: cream or stick foundation for the perfect zit cover-up. Then, just cover up what really bugs you and let your skin show through everywhere else.

How gorgeous are these girls?
You don't think, How gorgeous is the makeup?…

My kind of pretty:
Well-groomed, clean, fresh, glossy lip. What's the beauty message? They have their own personality, and they're definitely not trying too hard.

4. Sheer genius.

The perfect teen colors are sheer ones that you can see through. I like to use pale shades that look like natural washes of color on the face. Look for natural or soft pastel tones, nothing dark or bright. (P.S. These colors tend to be pretty mistake-proof, too.)

5. It's fine to shine.

I love shimmer shadows and lip gloss for teens—nothing looks more beautiful. The exception: Super

9. Avoid a makeup war.

As long as you are still a minor, your parents rule and still make the rules and you should try to be respectful of their wishes. But if they are saying "absolutely no makeup **ever**," it would be normal for you to want to sneak wearing a little makeup. If you choose to go against the rules, just be smart enough to go for something natural like brown mascara or pink lip gloss. Slipping out of the house in green glitter shadow was never easy for me!

YOUR BEAUTY MANTRA: SLEEP AND REST AND HAPPINESS AND HEALTHY LIVING MAKE YOU YOUR PRETTIEST.

shiny faces, which look good in fashion magazines but not on the face in the mirror. Don't try this one at home.

6. Dewey Is Awesome.

Think cream, not powder. When buying blush or shadow, look for a creamy formula—it looks more natural and goes on more easily.

7. It's only nail polish…

Bright orange? Army green? Metallic blue? Why not? It's inexpensive, easy to change, and fun to look at. The one color to skip (forever)? Black—it's plain ugly.

8. Shop around and mix it up.

Your local dime store's $1 bin is perfect for glitter and glam, but you may want to invest a little more money in your skin-care products and concealer.

10. Never say never.

Keep an open mind about new ways to wear makeup. Maybe you're not a red lip kind of girl...but what about sheer gloss in just the right red? That might be just gorgeous.

ROLE MODELS

You need one. I need one. We all need role models. And, whether we like it or not, we are presented with role models every single day of our lives. The

COOKIE-CUTTER BEAUTY IS BORING.

girl on the cover of a magazine, the actress in this season's hot movie, the lead singer of the all-girl band, the model in the makeup ad—all of these girls are role models. But not necessarily role models that we would choose ourselves.

My challenge to you? To find a beauty role model in your life. Someone whose style you admire. Someone whose look you'd like to emulate.

BE EXACTLY WHO YOU ARE!!!
SUPERMODELS ARE FREAKS OF NATURE!!!

Someone who, maybe even in the faintest way, looks somehow like you (i.e., Think again before you choose Naomi Campbell as your role model if you look more like Kate Moss).

When I was thirteen, the biggest role model was Cheryl Tiegs—tall, blond, blue eyes, straight hair, skinny, skinny, skinny, and "all-American." This wasn't great for my self-image since I didn't look anything like her and never would. She was not exactly my mirror image or that of my peers either. I remember with great happiness when *Love Story* came out (rent this movie if you've never seen it! Make sure you have plenty of tissues handy) with

the most incredible brunette beauty Ali MacGraw. Ahh. I was overjoyed! It was as if someone decided that brunettes could be pretty, too. Then along came a brunette model named Esme and, little by little, things began to change. Black models appeared for the first time on the cover of magazines. Still today, unfortunately, it's an event when a black girl is on the cover of *Vogue*. But where the early girls had "whiter" features, today black models really do look black. Alec Weck and Kiara, are two gorgeous black models.

Then came the explosion of "global" beauty—Asian, Indian, and Latin beauty was celebrated and actually preferred over the blond "all-American" role model I grew up **not** relating to…The next step after global was "interesting" beauty—freckles, strong noses, pale skin, and unusual features became the in thing.

So where are we now? It's a time of diversity of looks. No one ideal is being celebrated in the modeling world. And, thankfully, models aren't the only celebrities around anymore. The world is looking away from the runways and toward Hollywood and the rock scene for its icons. I think this is a refreshing change because it recognizes that developing a passion can only make you more interesting and beautiful.

03 SKIN CARE

It's never too early to begin thinking about your skin. Like brushing or flossing your teeth, your skin-care routine should become automatic. Everyone benefits from good skin care—men, babies, children—but especially teenagers. The same hormones that cause hair to grow under your arms and your period to start also crank up the oil-production levels on your face, which can trigger the biggest beauty bummer of teenagedom: zits.

H-O-R-M-O-N-E: This is a word that will stay with you throughout your life. Hormones are responsible for PMS (lovely) plus that once-a-month blemish that appears on your cheek just before you get your period. Hormones are also responsible for much more serious acne that can be frustrating, embarrassing, and even overwhelming. (*See chapter 6 for the whole scoop. Of course I dedicated an entire chapter to zits!*)

The most important thing to learn about your skin is that so much about its appearance and condition is determined by your parents and your genes. If your mother or father has beautiful, smooth, even skin, you're in luck…but that doesn't mean you are in for a free ride. You still have responsibilities to

AN IMPORTANT THING TO REALIZE IS THAT WHAT YOU PUT *IN* YOUR BODY IS MORE IMPORTANT THAN ANYTHING THAT YOU PUT *ON* YOUR FACE.

care for your body and face. You can throw all the good skin out the window if you blow it by not taking care of yourself.

Hormones: They kick in when we hit puberty and are to blame for zits and PMS.

GOOD NEWS:

TAKING CARE OF YOURSELF = GOOD SKIN

Your skin will look its best if you:

• Eat healthy foods.

• Drink lots of water (8 to 10 glasses or 1.5 liters/day—carry around bottled water to get in the habit of drinking throughout the day). It gives you energy and gives skin a nice glow.

• Get good exercise (the kind that makes you sweat).

• Don't smoke or drink.

THE SUN

All You Need to Know About SUN CARE

A little sun looks good—too much looks burnt-out and old-fashioned. Besides, you'll regret it later when your skin becomes leathery and lined.

SPF 15 is the key to smart sun care. With a sun protection factor of 15, you will be protected from the harmful rays of the sun but still be able to get nice color over time. Anyway, no decent tan ever happened in a day, so why risk an ugly, painful burn? If you're impatient for color, use a bronzer or self-tanner. (Remember: Pale is so pretty with a soft pink blush.)

SUN FACTS

• TWO SERIOUS BURNS BEFORE THE AGE OF 18 DOUBLES YOUR CHANCES OF GETTING SKIN CANCER IN YOUR LIFETIME.

• Sunblock products are fully effective for only one year. Check for a date on all products, because after a year, you won't get total protection.

• Lips burn easily (the mouth has the thinnest skin on the body, and it burns the fastest!). Protect with SPF 15 lip balm.

• Use SPF 30 for serious outdoor exposure—any activity at high elevations (skiing, hiking) and any activity near the water (sailing, waterskiing, fishing, canoeing, etc.).

• Start protecting your hands from too much sun early. You'll thank me later.

BODY ABUSE = BAD SKIN

SMOKING AND YOUR SKIN

I've seen the smoking habit ruin the pretty, fresh skin of young models. Smoking takes the vibrancy out of your face and creates:

(now)

Gray, ashy, dull-looking skin

Dark circles

(when you're older)

Dry, parched appearance

Cracked lips and gross little lines all around the

mouth. You won't be able to wear lipstick without it "bleeding" into these little smoker's lines (YUCK). Yellow teeth.

Whoever considers it cool or grown-up to smoke needs a lot more than cigarettes to seem cool. Risking your beauty, not to mention your health, is hardly worth it. Besides, what great guy would want to kiss a girl who smokes?

DRUGS, ALCOHOL, ETC.

I don't need to tell you how stupid and dangerous drugs are. (Do I?) Just in case you're wondering, besides robbing you of your self-esteem and a bright future, these illegal substances can be extremely rough on you inside and out. You'll look beat up and have no glow to your skin or sparkle to your eyes. Your skin will be dehydrated and malnourished. If you do drugs or drink to be cool, ask yourself: How cool is it to be ugly?

THE DRILL

Routine is everything with skin care. Pick your plan and stick with it. Don't give your skin any excuse to break out!

1. Cleansers: You choose, based on your skin type and personal preference
All-over oily skin: Use an oil-free cleansing gel. Choose one that doesn't dry out your skin.

Normal skin/T-zone oiliness: Use either a clear face soap (one without detergent) or a foaming cleanser.

Dry skin: Use a creamy cleanser that you rinse off.

2. Toners: This step offers extra insurance that your face is clean
Oily or normal skin in hot, humid weather: Use an astringent with witch hazel or a small amount of rubbing alcohol. Tip: Facial wipes are easy, quick, and disposable—a great way to clean your face when you're away from home. Great for taking off makeup, too.

Dry skin or normal skin in dry weather: Use a nonalcoholic "conditioning" toner.

3. Moisturizers
Oily Skin:
In the A.M., avoid moisturizers, especially in warm, humid weather. Use oil free sunscreen.
In the P.M., use moisturizing cream on dry spots, zits, and under eyes.

Normal skin:
In the A.M., use moisturizing lotion with SPF 15.
In the P.M., use moisturizing lotion—no SPF is necessary. Use an eye cream under eyes.

For dry skin:
In the A.M., use moisturizing lotion with SPF 15.
In the P.M., use creamy moisturizer (i.e., a product that contains less water) and an eye cream.

For extremely dry skin or extremely drying conditions (like skiing or hiking at high altitudes): Use face oil.

À LA CARTE SKIN CARE

Now for the fun part…beyond your daily skin-care routine, there are lots of ways to treat your skin. In this case, you need to pick and choose what's right for you and when you need it most.

Eye Cream: If you are curious about trying an eye cream, it's never too early to start. Use it only at night, though. Put it on your lips while you're at it, for a little extra moisturizing.

Pore-cleaning rub-off masks: Dense masks that roll off face when you rub really hard. These masks are a pain but leave skin really smooth.

Peel Masks: The fun masks that can be used all over or just on T-zone or chin (i.e., the troubled parts). Caution: These masks can be habit-forming since it's so much fun to peel them away.

Hydrating Masks: These are great for dry skin or for anyone who's just endured a long plane ride or a really, really late night out.

Clay Masks: For oily or blemished skin. But moisturize afterward—the point isn't to dry out your skin.

Exfoliator, or a grainy scrub: For that really, really clean feeling. For your face, find a formula that isn't too harsh so that you don't irritate your skin. (There are natural formulas—I love a honey-almond one—that are more gentle.) Don't use scrubs every day, and be sure to moisturize carefully after. On the body, you can use a loofah or washcloth as an exfoliator or a grainy cleanser. (*Also, see Bobbi's homemade salt scrub, below.*)

Loofah or sponge: Good for smoothing skin all over your body, but too harsh for use on your face.

Aha lotion: Great for exfoliating and keeping skin smooth. Start with a low concentration and increase if no burning or redness occur. Use only at night. Since skin is being constantly exfoliated, be certain to wear sunblock and avoid direct exposure.

Matifying lotion: A great help for oily skin or oily T-zones.

QUICK HOMEMADE HELP
Puffy eyes (from crying, or whatever): Slice a raw cucumber thinly and put rounds on top of lids; or steep teabags in hot water, let them cool, and put the moist bags on your lids.

Masks: calming, relaxing, and good for your face—who could argue? Do a mask at home when you are positive that you'll have at least thirty minutes to yourself. Below, the step-by-step instructions to follow:
1. Wash face with a grainy cleansing cream.
2. Apply a clay-based mask that has a pore-cleaning

formula. Dive into a fashion magazine or call some-one to chat with while you wait.

3. After around twenty minutes, rinse off with warm water. (You may need to use a washcloth to remove all the little bits.)

4. Put on your normal moisturizer.

BODY

Top-to-Bottom Care

Neck: You've got thirty years not to worry about it, but don't forget to apply sunblock here.

Arms: Dry skin on the back of arms is normal. (Little whiteheads on the backs of arms are actually a sign of dryness.) Wash with loofah or washcloth and moisturize with any rich cream (a hand cream works well).

Elbows: Scrub well in the shower, and moisturize afterward to avoid dark elbow syndrome. If you have this problem, try the classic remedy—cut a lemon in half and, while sitting at a table, stick one elbow in each half for at least ten minutes.

Butt: Use a loofah in the shower with liquid soap to smooth skin and avoid breakouts here (it's known to happen!).

Legs: I like to do a quick shave every day in the shower to avoid a big serious job and the nasty stubble feeling inside my jeans. When you shave, moisturize legs extra carefully.

Feet: Use a pumice stone on heels if they're dry. Coat feet in thick hand cream after shower.

Toes: If you hate the hair on your toes, trim it.

BODY SCRUB—Bobbi's Own Recipe

Mix a box of rock salt or Kosher salt with olive oil (1 cup) and a few drops of any essential oil (I love lavender!). Keep salt/oil mixture in a sealed container in your shower.

Use as a weekly all-over body scrub.

Watch out: Avoid using after shaving or if you have any paper cuts on your fingers. Salt burns!

BODY BASICS

Apply moisturizer to damp skin—just after you step out of the bath or shower.

This is the most simple and important thing I can tell you to get soft-all-over skin, but you'd be surprised how few women actually do this.

This is a great trick for speeding through the body lotion motion. Keep baby oil or body oil in a plastic spray bottle in the shower. Turn off the shower, spritz all over and then pat skin dry (don't rub) with towel.

- **Exfoliate your skin**: Choose your weapon.
For your body
    Washcloth, loofah, gentle scrub product
For your face
    Washcloth, facial scrub, masks, pore strips, etc.

04 THE PERFECT MAKEUP KIT

Portable Beauty: In Your Backpack

It's much cooler not to lug around your entire make-up kit. Try to focus on a few key items that will help you get through your day. Keep things in a separate zip-up makeup bag or pencil case so that they stay clean.

1. Pressed powder compact with mirror to fix T-zone shininess
2. Foundation to cover up pimples
3. 3-in-1 pencil for lips, eyes, and cheeks
4. Lipstick or pot of gloss

Definitely leave at home:

Eyelash curler and mascara—once a day is enough

AT HOME: VANITY LESSON

Should Possess:

- Cleanser, moisturizer
- Foundation (for zit cover-up)
- Zit medicine
- Tweezers, scissors
- Brown/black or blue/black mascara
- Eye shadow (1 to 2 light colors)
- Blush (a soft, natural color)
- Lip gloss or stain

Nice to own:

- Eyelash curler

- A set of makeup brushes
- Colored mascara (for fun)
- Tinted moisturizer
- Bronzing powder or gel
- Funky experimental colors (don't spend a lot of $$ here—these are throwaway items)
- Flavored lip glosses
- Nail polish—some sheer ones and some funky ones
- All-over shimmer for eyes, cheeks, or lips

DON'T BOTHER BUYING

- Makeup mirror—It's best to apply makeup near a window so that you have natural light.
- Magnifying mirror—Avoid, if possible, since it'll encourage picking at blackheads, pimples, etc.
- Train case for cosmetics—it's cute in the movies, but in real life it's more useful to put things in small zip-up plastic bags or zipper-up nylon containers.

HOW TO KEEP IT ALL ORGANIZED

An artist bin or fishing-tackle box is perfect for storing makeup.

INSIDE BOBBI's BAG:

(Surprise!) I've figured it out.

What makeup do I use myself? Well, I create my

own little palette to keep things as compact as possible. There are six spots for:

1. Concealer
2. Foundation
3. Blush
4. Lip stain or lip balm
5. Lip shimmer
6. Matte lip color

I also carry gloss and a perfume sample.

BOBBI's BIG BOX

When I do makeup for a photo shoot or the runway, I bring along my professional kit. Makeup artists should be able to do just about any look on any possible subject from what they carry in their kits. Makeup artists also pride themselves on having a clean, well-organized box…mine usually starts out that way…

The basics:

11	shades of foundation
6	shades of powder
4	shades of concealer
15	blushes, both cream and powder
40	eye shadows, both cream and powder
75	lip colors
20	pencils, eye and lip
6	mascaras
10	nail colors
20	glosses

Excitement Items: I also carry many of the following, depending on my assignment:

Crème pots and tubes of bold, shimmery color. Extra matte dense shadows.

Crazy lip, eye, and nail colors like lavender eye sparkle, silver eye glitter, false eyelashes, blue and green nail polish, burgundy mascara, etc.

Tools of My Trade:

Puffs, sponges, Q-Tips, makeup and nail polish remover, moisturizing creams, eyelash curler, tweezers, baby scissors

And...to keep me going:

Mints, water, power bars, gum, portable phone

SUMMER: HOT-WEATHER ESSENTIALS

- SPF 15 lip balm
- Oil control moisturizing lotion with SPF
- Oil-free cover-up/foundation
- Gel blush or powder blush
- Powder eye shadow

Avoid: Anything too creamy or shimmery—it'll melt!

WINTER: COLD-WEATHER BASICS

- A moisturizer that's one step richer than what you usually use:

  Go from oil-free lotion to moisturizing lotion;

  Go from moisturizing lotion to moisturizing cream;

  Go from moisturizing cream to a richer hydrating cream;

  Go from rich hydrating cream to a face balm
- Cream blush
- Cream eye shadow
- SPF 15 lip balm

Avoid: Powder formulas and anything too drying

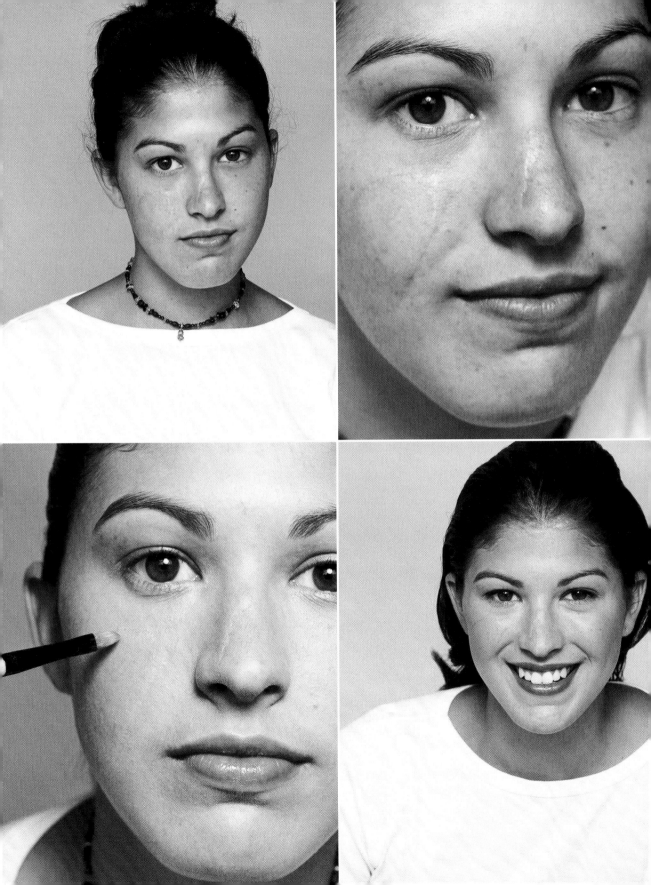

05 I HATE MY _____. (A LIKE-YOURSELF LESSON)

I've heard all the complaints. "I hate my strange nose." "I hate my big lips." "I hate my thin lips." What you can't stand is probably the thing I will find most beautiful about you. Distinctive characteristics are what makes a woman stand out and look pretty. And your own traits make you who you are. The sooner you get comfortable with this, the happier you will be.

I'm always surprised when I go to my high-school reunions. The prom queen who was every boy's dream and every girl's envy never looks so good. She looks tired, old. The best-looking girls are the ones I least suspected would become beauties—the quiet plain Janes who hadn't "blossomed" in their teen years but are now radiant. Girls peak at all different times. Growing up means finding yourself, and that happens at different moments for different people. The message? Appreciate what you've got when you've got it. If that means suffering through a little beauty envy in the short term, that's totally normal…as long as you don't let it take over your life!

Amanda Davenport, 15, Hedding, New Jersey
Self-conscious about: Scars on her face that she got in a car accident a year ago
"When this happened, I cried for a month. I thought my life was ruined. Now I am more comfortable

with the scars, but I prefer if people ask me about them rather than staring."

Amanda's mom helped her through the tough early days, telling her that she was still the same person and that her friends would still be her friends. Both of which proved to be true, although Amanda's probably a lot stronger now.

Bobbi's trick: Rather than using the gloppy scar makeup that Amanda was given after her plastic surgery, I applied stick foundation (in a yellow tone to match her skin), then I patted powder on top. The secret here, though, is the yellow tone—pink looks phony and pasty.

What Amanda never lost: Her big, gorgeous smile.

Julie Minsky, Sharon, Massachussetts
Hates: Her bushy eyebrows

Bobbi's message: Don't panic and pluck too much away. A strong brow is a great attribute—it frames your face and gives nice focus to the eye area. I cleaned up hairs between the two brows. Then I brushed them to the side and trimmed them slightly.

Beauty inspirations:

Brooke Shields, Mariel Hemingway

Aftereffect: "I like my brows a lot more now. Doing them isn't such a big deal."

Jen, 17, Kelowna, British Columbia, Canada
Hates: Her pale, pale white skin

Bobbi's message: Just go with it and give up on bronzers and suntans. Your snow white skin tone is

beautiful. Why would you ruin it trying to get a tan? Instead, wear pale pink blush—it'll make you look like an angel. Be proud of the paleness of your skin—it's one of the things that makes you special.

Beauty inspirations:

Kate Blanchard, Gwyneth Paltrow

Julie Ganison, 18, Hot Springs, Arkansas

Self-conscious about: The occasional pimple, wearing makeup

Bobbi's advice: Covering zits with concealer is the first step. But if you don't "seal" over the concealer with pressed powder, no blemish will be hidden for long.

Aftereffect: "I like looking natural. And I love finding a way to even out my complexion without that feeling of wearing makeup."

Beauty inspirations: Bobbi doesn't want to name names but she knows many, many famous models who always have major zits to cover.

SELF-ESTEEM ISSUES

When you don't look like Kate Moss...Or the one who happens to be the model of the moment. Your look just isn't THE look.

I grew up when the model "role model" couldn't have been more different than me: Cheryl Tiegs was tall, skinny, blond, and blue-eyed. My breakthrough moment was discovering Ali MacGraw, a brunette beauty I could relate to. My advice? Find a role model whose look relates to yours.

Standing Out: When You Don't Look Like Your Friends

Okay. It's tough. You are the only black girl in your grade, or maybe the only Asian girl in your school or neighborhood. How do you deal when blending in is the teenage goal. Your skin color or hair or features may be different, but your clothes and attitude can mesh with your peers. My advice: Be yourself and be true to yourself. If you are comfortable with who you are, those around you will be, too.

Moving: From New York, NY, to Ames, IA. Or, moving from Boise, ID, to Los Angeles, CA.

Going from a really sophisticated place where everyone has all the latest clothes and makeup to a really laid-back place where no one cares about the latest anything can't be easy. Doing the opposite move is just as difficult, or maybe even harder. The good news? People move all the time—you won't be the only new kid in the class. The bad news? It takes some time to adjust. A few guidelines.

1. Don't be clueless.

You'll learn a lot about your new school's beauty and fashion look just by observing. Do they wear jeans, khakis, or cargo pants? Are they new or old? Tight or baggy? Long or short? Do they wear their hair long or short? Do they wear sneakers or heels? Once you get the local style picture, decide what style would make you feel best. It's not about copying—just clue yourself in for inspiration.

2. Do something you like to do.

If you have special interests, sign up. Join the band, soccer team, or drama club. It's the best way to start developing acquaintances and making friends.

3. Find one friend.

Try connecting with one person who seems like good girlfriend material. And remember to be a good friend to this "first friend" even when, after six months, you have dozens of "best" friends.

4. Be cool.

Of course you feel insecure, but you don't have to show it.

Ugly Duckling: My older sister is sexy and beautiful and looks just like my mom. Somehow I got the UGLY gene.

I know how you feel. When I was growing up, my mom was amazingly beautiful, young, and skinny. None of her clothes ever fit me: She wore a size 2! That drove me crazy.

The fact is that we all peak at different moments. I peaked at thirty! There is no such thing as "ugly." Different, yes. Special, yes. Remember, you are **you**. Just be the best you can be.

NOSE JOBS, ETC. WHAT YOU NEED TO KNOW.

Plastic surgery: What an awful term. Plastic implies fake and surgery…**ouch**! Reconstructive surgery after an illness or accident is a great thing. But choosing to undergo a permanent surgical procedure to change a nose, chin, breast, or whatever is a decision that needs to be totally thought out.

If you haven't noticed already, **I L-O-V-E strong noses**. For me, a strong nose gives character to the face and its special beauty. You should know that you may "grow into" your nose. We all go through awkward physical times when our noses or chins haven't completely grown into our faces. But if nothing I can say will make you like your nose and you are really, truly miserable, then you might consider doing something.

Making them bigger: Give yourself a few years before you make this decision. Breasts can grow larger even in your early twenties. Be aware that implants only last ten years so this is not a "permanent" solution.

My honest advice? Wait. Don't do it for a boyfriend. Build your pectoral muscles and you'll feel better about your chest and be more able to wear low-cut clothes.

Liposuction: Isn't as easy as it seems. It hurts a great deal. It's expensive and is **not** recommended for teens. You can lose fat much less painfully by

YOU SHOULD BE TRULY MISERABLE
BEFORE YOU MAKE A PERMANENT CHANGE!

Be patient. The youngest possible age I'd recommend even considering it? Sixteen.

Breasts: Girls with big boobs want them smaller and girls with small ones want them bigger. (Welcome to the world, girls!)

Making them smaller: If you have gigantic breasts (here we're talking DDs and bigger) and are uncomfortable, you might think about doing a reduction. I've known a few teenagers who've made this decision. Was it painful? **Yes**. Was it expensive? **Yes**. Was it worth it? They have all said yes. Just make sure you really want to take this step. Don't do it unless you are at your ideal body weight. Often as you lose weight your bra size goes down.

exercising and cutting down on fat in your diet (*see chapter 12*).

Injections: Botox…silicone…**no no no**!!!!

Mole Removal: There are two sides to this story. Cindy Crawford chose not to have her mole removed, and it turned out to be one of the reasons she became the supermodel that she is. I, on the other hand, wish I'd had it done earlier. I waited till I was twenty one. I regret having waited so long since the mole made me really unhappy. If it bothers you, do something about it.

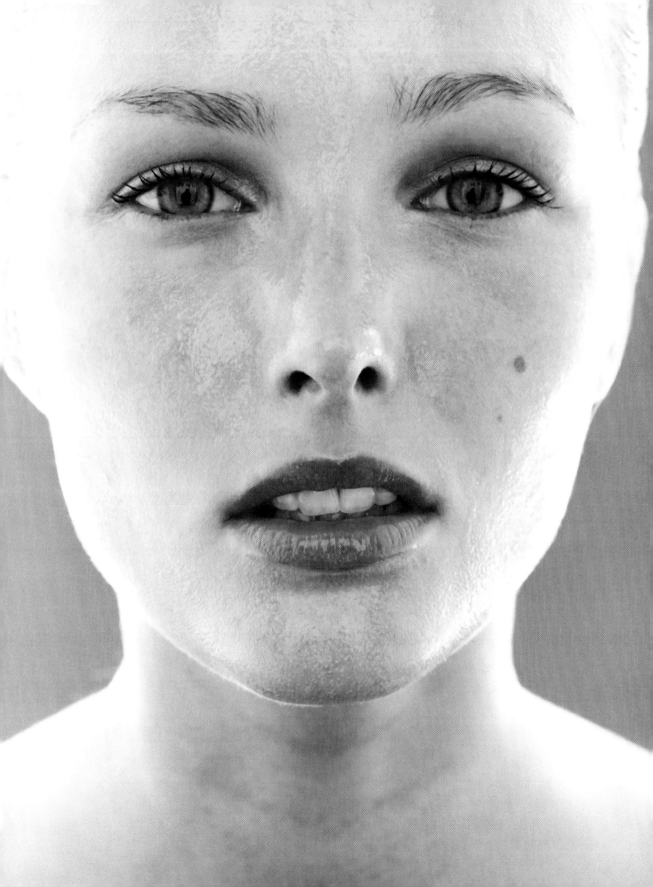

06 ZITS!

Zits: Teenagers' biggest beauty bummer. If you've got them and hate them, you are not alone. I wish I had an easy way to get rid of them, but there isn't one. I do believe that by eating healthy foods and drinking lots of water you can help prevent pimples. But it's also a question of genes—some girls are luckier than others with their skin, just as some are naturally thinner than others.

THE ZEN OF ZITS

Be zen about your zits. Instead of picking or attacking them, let them be…they will heal faster, and you'll be less likely to face permanent scarring. This is one of the hardest things to do in the world, but nothing will help your skin more. Hands **off**. Fingernails **out**!!!!

GETTING SERIOUS HELP

If your zits are making you miserable, and nothing you do seems to make a difference, you should talk to your parents about seeing a dermatologist. A skin doctor has lots of options open to him or her in treating acne today. Even the most severe cases can be treated completely.

When to go to a derm: When you are close to despair…when your parents agree…when you have a seriously infected pimple or other acute condition.

What to expect: The doctor will want to take a close look at your skin through a lighted magnifying lens. Bring along what you have been using on your face to show the doctor. When you discuss solutions, ask specifically what you should be using to wash, tone, and moisturize your skin. If the doctor prescribes a lotion or an antibiotic, get clear information about when to apply it or when to take the medicine. Ask if there are foods you should avoid. Be prepared to get as much information as you can. Doctors are busy people—get the most out of your ten minutes with yours. (You are paying for it!)

How to find the best doctor: ask around—friends, mothers of friends. Or ask your pediatrician, she or he is likely to know the best acne dermatologist in your area. (*See Index, page 196, Going to the Derm.)*

FOOD & ZITS

Doctors don't agree on whether certain foods cause zits. And everyone is different so it's nearly impossible to pinpoint zit-causing foods. Some people think chocolate and Coca-Cola cause pimples. Maybe it's the caffeine in both. It seems logical that greasy fried foods (French fries, onion rings, etc.) might contribute to the problem. Others think that iodine-rich foods like shrimp, scallops, and lobster trigger breakouts. If you are aware of what you eat and when you break out, maybe you can figure out your own personal trigger foods. And then steer clear!

Don't forget that good nutritious foods can only help. Drink plenty of water. Vegetables and whole grains are total beauty foods!

THE ZIT-OF-THE-MONTH CLUB

If you get one nasty pimple every month a week or so before your period, you are a member, and you have your teenage hormones to thank. The worst thing about this monthly eyesore is that you never know where it'll pop up. Follow your cleansing routine religiously and be prepared with your blemish stick, tea tree oil, or other products that work for you. *Then see page 40 for cover-up help.*

THE GOODS: It's smart to keep a stash of useful products around so you can take action the minute you see trouble. Rather than picking it—**treat** it.

Cleanser: Start with the right formula for your skin. Oil-free if your skin is oily or broken out. Creamy if it's dry.

Grainy Scrub: Use weekly for smooth skin and to lift off dry patches. Make sure you buy a gentle formula and don't overscrub!

Tea Tree Oil: It's a natural astringent you can find at the health food store. Put a very light coat all over your face every night after washing and before you moisturize. (Be careful not to get it into your eyes.) Or, you can use it on a Q-Tip to dab spots directly.

Clay Mask: This is great for deep cleansing. It will clean your pores and help get rid of blackheads.

Peel-Off Mask: Who can resist? Pulling this mask off is so much fun! It helps exfoliate your skin, lifting off dry skin.

Blemish Stick: For the days when you face a serious zit, this is a medicated blemish medicine that you apply to the spot, several times a day.

Medicated Cover-Ups (like Clearasil): Be careful of tinted medicine sticks, because the color is usually horrible and they look pasty. I prefer to use untinted medicine and the perfect cover-up.

DON'T DRY OUT YOUR SKIN

There's a tendency to want to kill every germ on your face by using really strong zit medication. That's fine as long as you remember to moisturize afterward. Moisturizer (use oil-free if skin is super oily) helps skin breathe and contributes to the healing of skin. It also makes skin smoother, so it's a lot easier to cover them up: Flaky, dried-out zits are impossible to hide!

Steer clear of anything that will dry out a blemish, like drying soaps, cleansers, topical medication. These products won't help your skin in the long run.

COVER-UP vs. CONCEALER

Use cream or stick foundation as your **zit cover-up**. The most important thing is that it matches your skin color exactly.

Concealer is not for zits!!!! Unlike cover-up, concealer is lighter than skin tone and should be used on dark under-eye circles and at the dark inner corner of the eye. Putting concealer on zits will draw more attention to them because it will make them look too light.

Really important: Yellow tones are best and tend to look most like your skin tone.

Foundation all over your face will look too made up at this point in your life. And, besides, your skin doesn't need it. Use foundation only on zits. If you want some all-over cover, choose a tinted moisturizer because it's more sheer and natural.

SEE NO ZITS: STEP BY STEP

1. Spread oil-free moisturizer all over your face. Use your finger to pat a little extra moisturizer on zit and give it a second to absorb. (Here the idea is to have a **smooth** surface—not chafed or rough.)

2. Use your finger or a thin brush to cover zits with foundation. Over-rubbing or over-blending will simply remove all your coverage so don't overdo it.

3. Set with yellow-toned powder on a cotton powder puff. Wipe off excess with brush.

ZIT's STILL SHOWING!!

If you are not satisfied with your coverage, check these things:

Color: Does your zit really disappear on your skin when you go outside? Yellow tones are the key (both for foundation and powder). Shop hard for these products and beware: 90 percent of what's sold is pink. **Make sure that you try a product on your face and check in daylight before you buy it!** Here you'd be smart to shop in a department store where you can ask for help and sample colors.

Texture: Is the pimple dry because it's healing? Don't be afraid of moisturizing. Oil-free moisturizer won't make you break out more. I promise.

Size: Is the zit just too big and red to cover up? Don't touch it! Picking will make it more red and rough, and it will take longer to heal. Do the best job you can covering it up, and then put some fun color on your eyes or lips to take attention away from it!

WHEN TO OPERATE

Your parents or dermatologist will say **never**…but I know that there are desperate moments when you have to take action.

PIMPLES

Under **no circumstances** should you squeeze normal everyday pimples. You'll be so sorry. It will make them look horrible. Just cover them up fast and let them heal.

If a pimple is inflamed (hot) and buried under the skin, you may want to schedule an emergency visit to the dermatologist. In serious cases, the skin doctor may inject a major pimple with cortisone and it will disappear instantly. Don't run to the doctor with every zit, however, asking for a shot, because this procedure is expensive and it brings the danger of leaving permanent indentations.

WHITEHEADS

When you have a major, oozing whitehead and, because of it, you can't possibly go out in public, you might try the following before you go to bed:

1. Put hot (not scalding) water on the corner of a washcloth and press it **gently** to the spot.

2. Take your time and continue the above until the spot opens up and drains itself. Again, **be gentle**!

3. By the next day, the spot should be easy to cover.

BLACKHEADS

Generally I advise using a grainy scrub, washcloth, or loofah to help remove blackheads. But if you have a glaring, ugly one, you might try the following:

1. Take a hot, steamy shower.

2. As soon as you get out, **gently** squeeze, using two fingers on each side of blackhead. (Avoid digging nails into your skin—try to use the pads of your fingers.)

3. If it doesn't pop out immediately, wait until your next steamy shower. You can also go to a facialist—she knows how to do it right.

REMEMBER: YOUR PERCEPTION OF WHAT's ON YOUR FACE IS MUCH WORSE THAN THE REALITY. TRY TO FORGET ABOUT IT. SMILE. GET ON WITH YOUR DAY. IT's NOT WHAT EVERYONE ELSE IS NOTICING. (REALLY!)

07 EVERYTHING EYES

There's nothing more beautiful than clear eyes. Natural definition and innocence is a great gift when you are young. This is a time of your life when you don't actually need much makeup to make your eyes sparkle. But beware—too much of the wrong makeup will take away from your eyes.

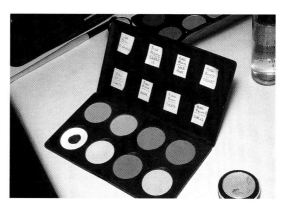

SHADOW

Experiment with light, fun colors—pastels, soft metallics, and brights.

Go beyond powder shadows for textures that are creamy, shimmery, sparkly, or glittery.

Break the rules and avoid perfection. What's modern in shadow is being casual with the color. Spread one shade all across one lid and don't worry too much if the other lid is slightly different. There are no rights and wrongs here. (This is probably one instance where the way your mother does it is not your blueprint.)

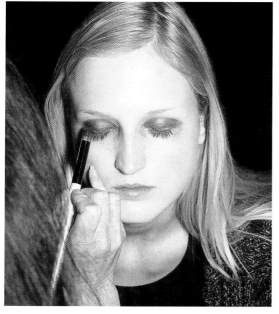

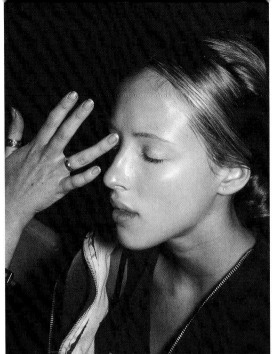

BIGGEST EYE MISTAKE

Trying to change the shape of your eyes with dark shadow (i.e., contouring)—all you'll end up doing is making your eyes look smaller. Contouring is a really advanced technique that some professional makeup artists haven't figured out. My advice? You don't need to change the shape of your eyes—they are pretty wonderful the way they are.

LINER

Too much will make you look like you tried too hard.

HOW-TO

Use a favorite shadow as liner. Smudge it around your eye. Sexy, smoky, and modern.

EYEBROW LESSON

Getting the right shape is everything when it comes to your eyebrows. When in doubt, leave yours alone—taking away too much is the worst thing you can do. Thick, natural, untouched brows are much more beautiful than overplucked, over-manicured brows.

To make sure your shape is natural-looking, you need to keep the natural shape of your brow. Just use your tweezers to clean up stray hairs.

Don't glue yourself to a magnifying mirror without coming up for breath. Stepping back and taking a look may save you from taking off too much. Over-plucking is most girls' biggest regret.

Finding Your Shape

1. Brow should start at the inner corner of your eye. Hairs should not cross into the unibrow area between eyes.

2. Brows should extend all the way to the outside edge of your eye.

3. The arch of your brow should be two-thirds of the way out.

BAD BROWS

The one eyebrow shape that's nowhere? The tad-pole brow, or hook-shaped brow...it gives you a puzzled look, and it looks old-fashioned.

Eyebrow Maintenance Kit

These are the three essential elements every girl needs for well-groomed brows:

1. Tweezers. Get your own. Look for a pair with a slanted edge.

2. Baby Nail Scissors. Use to trim long eyebrow hairs, which might be the only thing some girls need to do to clean up the area.

3. Wax. Yes. You can do it on your own to clean up the unibrow look. Or, go to a local salon that does waxing. It's best to get a recommendation from someone you trust, since they can wax too thin. In any case, be very careful. Discuss what you want before the wax goes on!

The Perfect Brow:

Not too narrow, not too short, with the perfect arch.

Too-short brow:

Makes eyes look small.

Big gap between brows:

Makes eyes seem narrow.

Tadpole brows:

Gives you a panicked expression.

08 BLUSH BASICS

THE PERFECT COLOR BLUSH IS THE SHADE OF YOUR CHEEKS WHEN YOU EXERCISE!

It's all about your color choice in blush—the right color should blend itself. If blush is too obvious, you've got the wrong one.

- If you have **very pale skin**, stick to **soft pastels** with no brown in them. (Brown can make your face look dirty.)

- If you have **light** skin, use **pale pinks**. If you have **medium skin**, use **sandy pinks**.

Before: Pretty and natural.

After: With blush—warm, pretty, and natural; a simple beauty look that's achieved with one strong element.

- If you have **dark** or **black skin**, choose deep, rich colors, like **soft plum** or **deep bronze**.

- If you have **yellow** or **olive skin**, look for shades like pink, tawny, or rose, and stay away from peach and bronze.

The wrong blush: It makes you look dirty, bruised, or pasty.

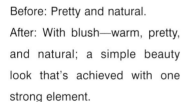

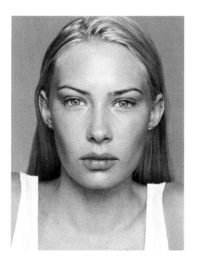

THE RIGHT FORMULA

There are so many blush options out there, I can understand if you get confused…

Powder: blush or bronzer

Powder is the easiest to apply, especially if it's the perfect shade. For blemished skin, stick with powder blush.

Cream: made in pots, sticks, and tubes
Cream blush looks the most fresh and natural, but you need to work on application. Blend it into your cheek, then turn your face to the side and blend it down. Skip this formula if you have oily skin. Skip cream blushes in the summer unless skin is super dry.

Pencils: all—in—one for lip, eye, and cheek. Blend carefully, as above.

Gels and Stains: sold in bottles or tubes
Gels and stains are great summer blushes for oily skin. Blend quickly and don't forget to wash your stained fingers!

SIMPLE APPLICATION
Smile…a big smile…Use your blush brush (see below) to apply blush to the beautiful apples of your cheeks. Blend up into hairline and blend down to blend with skin tone.

If you are worried that you've loaded too much blush on the brush and you want a really natural look, give brush a shake before applying. It's easy to add more later.

Emergency Blush: In a pinch (i.e., you need to brighten up your face but don't have your total kit with you), blend lipstick into your cheeks. Start with the smallest amount and blend well for a creamy blush look.

BLUSH BRUSH

It's nice to have your own full—cut blush brush, rather than using the thin ones that are sold with powder blush. A fuller brush makes a natural application easier since you can blend better.

09 LIPS

Lipstick is fun. Experimenting with it and playing with color is the quickest way to change your look.

Soft lips are what all girls want.

Full lips are sensuous and amazing. (The fuller, the better for me!)

Small, thin lips are also beautiful. They look best with lighter natural colors and lots of gloss.

How to Make Your Own Lipstick Palette

1. Buy an empty metal palette case with room for eight to twelve colors at a theatrical makeup store or beauty supply shop. (*See Index, page 195.*)

2. Use dental floss to cut the tips off your favorite lipsticks. Try to use as little as possible since you can always add more color later. For lipsticks that are almost all gone, use a baby spoon or caviar spoon to scoop up color from bottom.

3. Smush the color into an individual pan, blending it down.

4. Use a Q-Tip to clean up around pan.

NOTES

Some makeup artists striving for perfection melt lipsticks down in a low oven to get the cleanest-

looking palette. I prefer the "artistic" look of the handmade approach.

Some girls who are crazy for gloss, try to drop gloss into their palettes. I think that it gets too "gooey."

MIXING IT UP

The whole point of building your own lipstick palette is to be able to blend your own colors. There are some basic guidelines to mixing colors, but no absolute rules.

Technique: Mix colors together on the back of your hand using a lip brush. This is the technique I use with models, but when blending on myself, I do it directly on my lips. It's not as messy, and it's faster.

Start with either a light or dark shade. It doesn't matter which goes on first since you can adjust later on.

Too dark? Blot with tissue and layer on lighter shades like white, beige, or pink.

Too light? Build up darker shades like blackberry, which magically turns almost any lip into an evening look.

Too intense? Use **beige** to mute almost any color (white, on the other hand, makes colors look pasty).

Too blah? Use red to brighten—but use sparingly.

LIP TRICKS

Use lip pencil and lip balm to create your own color.

Use eye shadow and lip balm to create a matte lipstick. Watch out, though, when choosing your shadow color—most are too gray or brown.

Make a great stain by applying a bright or dark shade, then blotting most of it off.

To make lip color last longer, use lip pencil on top of lipstick.

Most modern mouth: Sheer colors are the most modern and mistake—proof. Try either pots or tubes.

10 BEAUTY SCHOOL 101

Caroline Eggert from Arkansas helps me demonstrate the basics. She's perfect for me since she has strong natural features: thick brows and full lips.

EIGHT SIMPLE STEPS TO A PRETTY, NATURAL MAKEUP LOOK

Once you get the hang of this process, you'll be able to whip through these steps in just a few minutes. For more instruction on each topic, check out the chapters noted below.

Prep: Face is clean and you've applied moisturizer *(see chapter 3—skin care)*.

Step 1: Cover dark circles

With your index finger, gently smooth concealer that's one shade lighter than your skin under the eye to cover any darkness there *(see concealer lesson, chapter 6)*.

Step 2: Cover zits and redness

If you have blemishes, use foundation that's the exact color of your skin to cover. Use your finger or a brush.

Step back from the mirror and check whether you have any blotches or redness. Use foundation to cover *(see chapter 6)*.

Step 3: Sealing your coverage

Using a powder puff, pat a small amount of powder

lightly over face to set your makeup. Skip this step and your cover-up will disappear! (*see chapter 8*). Warm tone powder works best.

Step 4: Don't forget your brows

Comb your brows up and across using a brow brush or a toothbrush (one that you've bought just for this purpose!) (*see chapter 7*). Or softly apply shadow to fill in brows to make fuller.

Step 5: Shimmerize your lids

Use your finger or a brush to apply a shimmery shadow to the eyelid. Here I used a silvery lavender shade that looks good on almost everyone (*see chapter 7*). Experiment with colors and after texture.

Step 6: Natural Flush

Cream blush goes on the apple of your cheeks (*see chapter 8*). Blend up and down.

Step 7: Lusher Lashes

Mascara goes on top and bottom lashes—thicker on the outer lashes (*see chapter 7*). Do one or two coats and let it dry in between.

Step 8: Lastly, Lips

Fill in entire lip using a creamy lip pencil. Then, using your finger or brush, spread gloss on top (*see chapter 9*). Experiment with colors and textures.

11 CLIFFS NOTES BEAUTY TEENAGE MASTER CLASS

TWENTY MOST-ASKED QUESTIONS

HERE'S YOUR OWN CLIFFS NOTES BEAUTY: FAST HELP+WHERE TO TURN FOR MORE INFO.

To compile these "biggest beauty mysteries," I pulled together a group of girls—friends and friends of friends. City girls, suburban girls, and even a couple of country girls. Their ages? Barely teenage to college girls. At the beginning, everyone was shy and no one admitted their beauty fears or frustrations. By the end of our two-hour session, everyone was gushing with problems for me to solve. I asked for an honest, open forum and got it. You can sit in and listen (and I'm sorry I can't offer you the Diet Cokes, carrot sticks, and brownies these girls put away).

Q: What's the best way to calm a breakout on the night before the prom?

A: Herbal tea—like chamomile—drink it to calm down. And remember—you are not in total control. Just do your best with cover-up tricks (*see chapter 6*) and try to have fun. Otherwise…what's the point?

Q: What's the best way to hide zits? —Jessica, 16

A: Anything white or light applied to the skin makes the area more noticeable. (Think how a white skirt makes you look fatter than a black one.) Match your skin tone exactly with stick or creamy foundation, and use as your concealer. Apply with your finger in a patting motion. If pimple is dry to begin with, put on an oil-free moisturizer first. Making a zit look smooth is key. Going out with a cakey-looking covered-up zit is the worst (*see chapter 6*).

Q: At what age can I start lightening my hair? —Rebecca, 18

A: Salon coloring is expensive and time-consuming. And I don't recommend doing permanent coloring at home. But eighteen is certainly old enough to find a colorist whom you like, if that's how you want to spend your money. Some other home-lightening possibilities: You can do a lemon spritz now to lighten naturally. Or do a blonding shampoo or temporary color (*see chapter 26, Hair*).

Q: How should a girl go about tweezing her brows? —Lara, 15

A: Tweezing is serious business—it's smart to think before you attack. It's also smart to tweeze just after a shower so it doesn't hurt. Tweeze between your brows and clean up stray hairs, plucking from beneath your brow line. The other option? Having your brows waxed at your local salon. Just make sure they don't take off too much (*for total details, see chapter 7, Eyes*).

Q: What can I do about my shiny skin? —Bridgette, 16

A: The good news is that your skin will look younger longer. The bad news is you have to deal with it now. Try using a shine-control product on your oily zones during the day. Apply powder to these same areas using a powder puff. Use an oil-free moisturizer at night. You might want to buy some thin paper blotters (they come in a little book—Estee Lauder sells them) and carry them around with you in hot weather (*see chapter 3, Skin*).

Q: What can I use to cover "café-au-lait" spots on my neck?

A: If spot is lighter than your skin color, mix together a slightly deeper foundation than you usually use. Apply it only on the spot and pat warm toned powder (using a puff) on top. If spot is darker than skin tone, lighten it up with your concealer and yellow powder.

Q: How can I make my eyes look bigger? —Jessica, 16

A: Line them. The trick is to line close to the lashes. I love deep-set eyes like yours. They look great lined (*see chapter 7, Eyes*).

Q: How do you get rid of dark circles? —Gretchen, 18

A: Be sure you find yellow-toned concealer—it can't be pink! Then pat pale yellow powder over the top (*see chapter 6*).

Q: What makeup should I wear that won't make me break out more? —Sarah, 13

A: Makeup doesn't make your skin break out. (Hormones are the biggest cause of breakouts. Not cleaning your skin properly, not eating right, not drinking enough water, and not sleeping enough also contribute to bad skin.) If you do break out, wear oil-free moisturizer. If you want to wear a foundation, find a tinted moisturizer—it's the lightest formula. Or, better yet, just use concealer to cover spots and don't wear all-over makeup.

Q: If I wanted to be a makeup artist like you, where should I start?

A: Have fun practicing makeup on your friends and family. Volunteer to do the makeup for a school play. Check out whether the community theater in your town needs extra help backstage. Or find a local makeup artist whose work you admire. Offer to work as his or her assistant so that you can learn. No matter how serious you think you are about being a makeup artist, I advise finishing school before you go pro. I graduated from college and I'm grateful that I did (and that my father pushed me through!).

Q: When I have a bad face day, should I wear my same makeup?

A: Blush is instant prettiness! *(See chapter 8, Blush.)*

Q: How can someone with bad acne still feel confident about herself?

A: Learn to be a master painter and you'll find yourself obsessing less about your imperfections *(see chapter 6, Zits).*

Q: Is it bad for girls to share makeup? —Amanda, 14

A: Wipe down a friend's lipstick with tissue before you use it. If you keep your hands absolutely clean, you can share almost anything else that you apply with your fingers.

Q: My nose is huge and I don't know what to do. Help! —Marianne, 16

A: If your nose is strong and distinctive, it's part of your personality and, chances are, you'll grow into it. If, however, your nose is truly out of proportion with your face (and you are at least sixteen), talk to your parents about consulting with a plastic surgeon. But I really hesitate exploring this route. Do so **only if you are really miserable**! A nose job is painful and it takes months and months for the swelling to go down. What's more: It's permanent—there's no going back! *(See chapter 5.)*

Q: Will my boobs ever grow? —Laura, 13

A: It's impossible to say when your boobs will "pop" or how big they'll ultimately be. Growth can continue well into your early twenties. As impatient as you are now, try to relax about it. Small boobs are more the look, and are easier to do sports in and wear clothes over. More women will complain about big boobs than small later on in life. Average size is 34B. Doing push-ups will help develop your pectoral muscles, and that will make you feel better about your chest. Wearing the right bra can make a big difference, too. Go with your best friend to visit the lingerie department of a good department store and experiment with different styles.

Q: What's the right shade of eye shadow for me? I have a hard time finding a shade that looks right. —Julia, 14

A: In choosing eye shadow, consider the texture as well as the color. Shimmery shadows are nice for teens (and easier to apply). Since you look pretty

in blue, try a light shimmery shade of blue. Then, just wear a hint of it—you can control the intensity of color by how much you put on (*see chapter 7, Eyes*).

Q: Is there a way to wear red lipstick so it doesn't look like I'm trying too hard? —Maria, 19

A: Try mixing a small amount of red lipstick with clear gloss. What do you get? See-through red lips that are young and pretty.

Q: I hate my frizzy hair. What's the trick to blow-drying it yourself? — Sara, 12

A: Do you really have to blow it dry all the time? What would happen if you wore it naturally? Next time you wash it, put in some leave—in conditioner and let it dry naturally. Don't touch it; that just makes it frizzier (*see chapter 26, Hair*).

Q: I hate the way my hair sticks to my lip gloss, what can I do? —Alyssa Samson, 12

A: Don't wear lip gloss! Instead, try lip balm or Chap Stick. Avoid Carmex (and similar products that contain camphor) because it dries cold sores and your lips. Another solution: Put your hair in a ponytail.

Q: What's the best way to wear shimmer? I love it on my lips and eyes, but not on my face. —Teagan, 14

A: There is such a thing as shimmer overload. And having a shiny face, glossy lips, and shimmery eyes definitely qualifies. Even though shiny faces look beautiful in magazines, **don't try this at home**. It'll just look like your face is oily. Do your lips and/or eyes and keep your face natural.

BEAUTY ROLE MODELS

Picking a star version of yourself is good inspiration.

When I asked the girls at my Cliffs Notes forum if they had beauty role models, they all said yes. Their choices were so great that I'd like to show them off.

Teagan Leahy relates to **Natalie Portman**. Both are small and have a sweet brunette beauty.

Emily Silver connects with **Sarah Michelle Gellar**. A natural beauty role model.

Jessica Shaw likes **Drew Barrymore**. A great pairing—they both have round faces and love kicky makeup.

Sara Covey likes **Julia Roberts**. Totally on—they both have great smiles, full hair, and strong bone structure.

12 YOU AND YOUR BODY
STYLE, FOOD, AND EXERCISE PLANS FOR EVERY BODY TYPE

Bobbi's Bod…Bobbi's Style

I would love to have been born with a different body type. Taller, definitely, with longer legs and leaner-looking—but none of that was in the cards for me. I have learned to buy simple-fitting clothes that make me look like I am all those things. But it's taken me years to come to that clothing realization. In high school I wore high platforms, long dresses, and middle-parted hair streaked with gold and as long as it would grow. Since then, I have learned that simple shoulder-length (or shorter) hair works better for a person my size (all 5'0" of me!). Shorter skirts make my legs look longer. And I sometimes wear heels that definitely make me look taller. But most often you'll find me happy and comfortable in flats. I *love* wearing my penny loafers.

Each of us has her own body thing—too tall, too short, too fat, or too thin. **It's hard to find a female on this planet who's totally happy with her body.** But, instead of torturing yourself over what it is you do not like, be realistic about what you can and cannot change. Yes, it's possible to gain or lose some weight. And, yes, like billions of other women, I would like to be five to ten pounds thinner. Although it's not possible to make yourself taller or shorter, how you dress and carry yourself can send out a totally different perception of your size. I will never stop watching my diet or exercising but I will never let myself get totally miserable about it either. That's not productive. Why dwell on the negative stuff you can't change? I find it's better to just let go…

IF YOU'RE BIG

Role models: Emme, Camryn Manheim, Rosie, female hockey players

Remember: Some girls were just not meant to be thin. Big bones and a meaty frame can be beautiful and sexy. Lots of guys are attracted to larger women. Latin men are known to prefer voluptuous bodies over rail-thin model types. The important thing? **Accept yourself. Stop fighting yourself, and be healthy!**

But self-acceptance shouldn't be an invitation to pig out on junk food. Try to eat only healthy foods and avoid those empty, non-nutritious calories.

WHAT'S YOUR MASTER PLAN FOR DEALING WITH YOUR WEIGHT?

Food: I hate the idea of dieting because it's so easy to cheat. (It's human nature.) It's smarter to change the way you eat altogether without severely limiting what you eat. If you simply eliminate sweets, obvious bad stuff (like doughnuts, fries, pizza, and sodas), you may find that you drop the extra weight pretty painlessly. I believe that if you eat balanced meals and healthy snacks, your body will find its own comfortable weight.

If you are at least 20 pounds overweight, see what Dr. Ruden has to say (*see page 197*). You might need to see a pediatric nutritionist or find a weight-loss program in your community.

Exercise: Find some comfy exercise clothes and go take a spinning class, try kick boxing, or just go for a walk. Sometimes the best thing is to get outside and **move**—try starting a walking/jogging program with your mom or a friend. To see change, you'll need to do something active four or five days a week.

What to wear: Solid colors. You can't go wrong with simple silhouettes and classics like jeans, turtlenecks, polo shirts.

What Not to wear: Anything too tight or too short. Big prints, ruffles, and pleats are a bad idea. So are leggings.

Treats: Buy great-looking sandals and have a professional pedicure. Keep your hair and makeup pretty.

IF YOU'RE UNHAPPY ABOUT 5 TO 10 EXTRA POUNDS

Role models: your mother (probably), me (sometimes), and most models, girls, you know.

So… you want to lose five to ten pounds….Join the club. It's normal to gain five or so pounds during final exams, the holidays, or vacations. And, I am sorry to tell you, this kind of periodic weight gain is probably going to be a normal thing for the rest of your life. The best thing to do is not go crazy. When you eat more, you tend to retain more water in your body. (So all the extra pounds are not fat!) Don't beat yourself up. Get through finals week or enjoy the holidays or spring break, then get yourself back to healthy eating. You'll feel like yourself again in a couple of days.

For times when I feel a little heavy, I put aside some flattering pants and shirts that I know will make me feel good. Bad mirror feedback is the worst!

Let's talk about our world's **distorted body image** for a second. Most of us think we have ten to fifteen pounds to lose because we are constantly exposed to unrealistically skinny body images in magazines, movies, MTV, and those teenage TV shows. Can everybody really be that thin? No, no, no. But the models and actresses in the magazines and on TV shows are really thin. For some, it's easy, and totally natural. For others, looking thin and perfect is a struggle. The pressures of this life (there's always someone thinner and prettier about to be discovered!) sometimes lead to drug or alcohol problems, or plain unhappiness.

You also need to remember that whenever you see a picture of a perfect model, there has been an army of professionals who worked to get her that way…hair stylists, makeup people, wardrobe people…You'd look amazing, too.

The message here is that models on the covers of fashion magazines are not reality. I guarantee it (I've been there!). These "perfect" girls have their dark circles, pimples, fat days, bad hair days just like you do. We **all** do. There is a team of people working to create a perfect image. The pimples, dark circles, and frizzy hair vanish, thanks to their help.

And let's not forget the **retoucher** (ever heard of airbrushing?)—zap on the computer and everything is cleaned up and thinned out—arms, legs, thighs…

Model thin isn't necessarily **pretty**! Be healthy, be strong, be yourself!!

IF YOU'RE NATURALLY THIN

Role models: Courteney Cox Arquette, Gwyneth Paltrow, Cameron Diaz, Calista Flockhart

Some girls, believe it or not, are naturally extremely thin. They have naturally high metabolisms and fight to keep weight on. If you qualify and were born-to-be-thin, just remember that we are all jealous.

Strategy for healthy weight gain: drink milk shakes, have frequent small meals, and carry around nuts and raisins for snacks.

Exercise: You need to do weight-bearing exercise to strengthen your muscles and give your body a stronger look. You can buy a set of weights (start with two or three pounds) and start doing basic arm exercises or ask for help at the weight room at your high school or local gym.

Clothes: You'll feel too skinny in head-to-toe tight clothes. Choose to wear tight jeans or a tight tee—not both. Have fun with colors and prints. White jeans are a great option (winter or summer). Layering gives you a little extra bulk...try wearing a jean jacket over a sweater or sweatshirt over a tank. But don't complain—most of us would happily trade.

IF YOU'RE SHORT

Role Models: Christina Ricci, Drew Barrymore, Paula Abdul, Jennifer Love Hewitt

Exercise: For a long, lean line, you'll want to do something aerobic, along with lots of stretching. Take an aerobics class or run one day, then do ballet, yoga, or a stretch class the next. Balance the two types of workouts.

Clothes: Simple, clean lines. Nothing too complicated. What works: the same color (dark) top and bottom, long straight skirts, long straight pants. What doesn't: thick belts.

Shoes: It's so tempting to wear heels or platforms all the time. Just be sure the shoes fit well so you'll still be happy at the end of the day. If your grandmother ever told you not to wear the same shoes every day, I agree.

IF YOU'RE TALL

Role Models: most models, most actresses, and basketball players

You are extremely lucky (even if you don't feel it just yet). You'll never have to hem a pair of pants and you'll look elegant in almost everything.

The boy thing: Don't worry if you are taller than your date. Who cares? On the other hand, I'd avoid wearing super high shoes—you don't need them.

Exercise: Make sure you develop postural muscles (i.e., avoid the tall-girl-with-slumped-shoulders look —it's never pretty) with weights, yoga, ballet, etc.

Join your school's volleyball, track, or basketball teams—they'd love to have you!

Clothes: Belts, hip-huggers, whatever…you can wear it!

BOBBI'S-BEING-GOOD:
BASIC HEALTHY-EATING PLAN

In a perfect world, I would eat only healthy foods all the time. But there are just too many temptations out there. So…instead of beating myself up after eating some rich, disgustingly delicious dessert (chocolate soufflé with chocolate sauce, for example), I promise myself that **tomorrow** I'll jump back into my healthy-eating plan.

Breakfast
Yogurt, fruit, toast *or*
Oatmeal, fruit, glass of milk, or soy milk *or*
Egg white Omelet (my favorite)

Snacks
Cottage cheese on rice crackers *or*
Almond or peanut butter on whole-wheat crackers

Lunch
Turkey sandwich on whole-wheat bread with light mayonnaise
Fruit or a fruit "leather" (you can find in health food stores)
1 or 2 fruit-sweetened cookies (ditto) *or*
One slice of pizza (If I can't order vegetables on top, I'll use napkins to wipe off all the excess oil)
Salad
Fruit

Dinner
Protein (here I mean broiled or baked chicken, fish, turkey, hamburger, or a steak)
Vegetable
Rice or Potato
Fruit
Dessert, either health pudding, health cookie, or a frozen yogurt

BOBBI'S FRIDGE POLICY:

Only put in it what you really want to put in to your body. Don't tempt yourself with junk or you'll eat it.

ALL SCREWED UP OVER FOOD

It happens a lot and it's very, very sad. Girls become obsessed over their bodies and stop seeing themselves clearly. They so desperately want to be thin and "perfect" that they stop eating almost completely (anorexia nervosa) or they eat only to purge the food out later by forcing themselves to vomit (bulimia). Unfortunately, eating disorders are a teenage reality in this country. They stem from psychological problems—feelings of worthlessness and low self-esteem—but, once addressed, can be treated. The first step to a cure is the ability to acknowledge a problem and confide in someone who loves you (best friend, sister, aunt, or mother).

Getting help: Admitting that there is a problem is sometimes the biggest step. Ask your doctor or school nurse for an eating disorder specialist in your community. Or just talking to your parents will greatly help—most likely they already know you have a problem and have waiting for you to mention it first.

13 PROM BEAUTY

OVERDOING IT IS THE WORST.

PERFECT PROM TIMELINE

One to three months before: Check magazines for the look you want. Then, shop for dress, then shoes and purse.

One month before (optional): Do a trial run with your whole look to make sure you like it. Make an appointment at your local salon to have your makeup, hair, and manicure done on prom day. Don't schedule anything later than 3 PM so that you leave plenty of time for yourself to get ready.

One week before: Try on dress with jewelry, shoes. Walk around your home to do a comfort check. If possible, take a picture of yourself in the dress to see if the look is working. Buy stockings. Shop for the perfect lip and nail colors.

One day before: Check that you have film for your camera. Do a trial run of makeup and hair look if you're doing it yourself. Prepare purse.

Prom day: Do a mask in the morning so your skin looks good. Try to do some exercise in the morning so you feel your best. Get to the salon on time. Wear a top that comes off easily so dressing later on doesn't mess up your face or hair.

Back at home: Eat a protein and carb snack just before you get dressed (like turkey on whole-wheat or an egg sandwich). **Why**?

1. to calm your nerves
2. to give you good energy
3. so you won't pig out later

Bobbi's advice: Wear comfy shoes!

Take tons of pictures and **have fun**!!! (Otherwise, what's the point?)

WAYS TO UP THE GLAM FACTOR

1. Shimmer shadow on eyes—play with pastels or silver-white or gold
2. Sheer shimmer dust on cheeks and shoulders
3. Rhinestones
4. Dark pencil, filled in all over lips and gloss over top
5. Pink sweater with a black sleeveless dress
6. Eyeliner: charcoal, navy, or brown
7. Bright or dark short nails
8. Red sheer lips
9. Hair up or back with fun barrettes
10. High shine lips
11. Strapless dress or tube top
12. Sequins
13. A metallic shoe
14. Bring along a colorful feather boa or fake fur wrap
15. Go for a sandal with a heel
16. Wear a tiara (really!)

Carry with you: breath mints, lip color, perfume tester, all-in-one compact, $ $ $, cell phone

THINGS TO AVOID ON A BIG NIGHT

- Getting a new haircut.
- Trying something tricky—like false eyelashes—for the first time.
- Getting complicated, hair-sprayed hair—you'll regret it later on when you are ready to get comfortable.
- Shoes that are totally ridiculous—do the stair test: if you can't go up and down a flight of stairs easily, forget it.

- Selecting a too-tight dress (if you're wondering whether it's too tight, it is).
- Using a makeup artist for the first time.

HAVING YOUR MAKEUP DONE PROFESSIONALLY: PROMS, WEDDINGS, AND OTHER SPECIAL EVENTS

This may sound strange coming from a makeup artist, but it's my advice that you do your own makeup. (After reading this book, you should be able to do a decent job.) Focus your energies and money on getting your hair done and getting a manicure. Keep your makeup light, natural, and pretty. But there may be moments in your life when you're asked to have your makeup done (like if you're in a wedding), and you'll not want too much old-fashioned makeup globbed on you. (No?) Here's how to get it right:

How to find a makeup pro
Go to your local department store. Look for a favorite sales associate at your favorite makeup counter. Ask that person for a quiet time when she or he can do your makeup: It should be free! (Good things to buy if you love the look? Special-effect makeup like sparkle shadow or glitter lipstick.) If you like what she or he does, see if that person is available to do a private appointment.

Otherwise, you can ask whether there is a resident makeup artist at your local hair salon.

When to trust someone
Explain that you'd like a polished, natural look—nothing scary or dramatic. Remember it's only makeup. You can always wash it off!

Best to avoid
Stay away from heavy foundation, too-serious contouring, overly done eyes. You won't want to be seen wearing old-fashioned makeup.

Having realistic expectations
Bring photos with you to help explain what you'd like.

Communicating your phobias without destroying makeup artist's creative space
Don't be afraid to speak your mind—the better you explain what you'd like, the bigger the chance you'll get what you want.

$$$
A private makeup job can cost anywhere from nothing to too much.

Always check prices before you say go!

Having a Beauty Party
Invite over a group of friends and get your makeup done together. Find a makeup artist you really like and organize a session at home with your best friends. Or, be your own makeup artists. Have your best pals bring over all their makeup and favorite makeup looks from magazines. Experiment! It's a good time to try new colors. Just don't swap mascara, just use your own.

14 PRETEEN BASICS

BEAUTY FOR ABSOLUTE BEGINNERS

There's no exact perfect age to start wearing makeup. Every girl has to decide for herself what's right and when she's ready. Basically, though, I think nine is too early (just enjoy being a kid, okay?) except for playing around with lipstick, blush, or nail polish at home with your friends. At twelve or so, you can start experimenting by wearing a little gloss or natural-looking mascara. Anything more than that I'd suggest saving for parties or dances.

SCHOOL RULE: DON'T DO ANYTHING BIG OR DRAMATIC. DO LIP BALM OR GLOSS AND A LITTLE BROWN/BLACK MASCARA. STOP THERE.

"What's the right age to start shaving my under-arms and legs? (My mother says it's too early.) How do I do it?"—Allison, 12

If your underarm and leg hair is coarse, thick, and dark, I can see why you want to shave. If, however, your hair is light and fuzzy, I'd recommend holding off since you don't want to be a slave to shaving…once you start, it's hard to go back.

A Girl's Guide to Shaving

1. Do it in the shower. The best way to shave is on wet skin. Wash legs and underarms first with soap and water to soften the hair. Turn off the tap or step to the side of the running water when you are ready to shave.

Before: Devon is completely adorable with a great smile and perfect bob.

After: A little gloss on the lips and brushed back hairstyle give Devon a more groomed look.

2. Use the thickest shaving cream you can find. I love the old-fashioned stuff (either buy your own or test-drive your dad's) because it's the thickest. In a situation where you can't get your hands on shaving cream, use hair conditioner—it works great.

3. Buy your own real razor and use a clean blade. Especially at the beginning, disposable razors are tougher to control and can leave your legs with ugly nicks.

4. Take your time and stay alert. Maybe an early-morning shower isn't the safest moment for you to be handling a razor.

Unwanted Hair: Options

Hair removal products: The spray-on type of hair removal products are stinky and a pain. No one I know uses them on a regular basis. Try another approach.

Laser Hair Removal: Dermatologists can perma-nently remove hair with a laser. This is a very expensive and time-consuming option that some women love. A popular use? The permanent perfect bikini line.

Waxing: Your local salon probably does waxing. It's great for a small area like the eyebrows or bikini line. Some women also like to wax their legs. But the price of perfectly smooth waxed legs is waiting the two long weeks for your leg hair to grow in. But I can't wait that long…that hairy feeling inside my jeans is enough to keep me from waxing my legs forever! And besides it hurts so much!!

"I have to get braces soon and I'm panicked. What can I do so that I'll still be considered pretty?"—Julie, 11

Just like with a new haircut, it may take a while for you to get used to braces. But just look at how great these girls look. Don't stop smiling (*for more info, see chapter 17, Braces*).

"I'm worried about where I'll be when I get my period. How can I avoid embarrassment?"—Grace, 10

It's totally normal to worry about this. When your period does arrive is a moment you will always remember. It comes when you least expect it and there is little you can do to prepare. The good news is that your first period will probably be quite light, so you will see or feel something before it shows. If you're in a pinch without a pad, use folded tissues or toilet paper.

"When should I start wearing deodorant? Is there something natural I can use that works?"—Nina, 12

If you are asking the question, you probably don't need to use a deodorant just yet. When you feel the need to start, shop around for a product that works for you. You should like its scent (or the fact it has no scent). Don't just settle for whatever you find in the medicine cabinet.

I like the natural deodorants that you can find at health food stores because they contain fewer chemicals. My favorite brand: Tom's of Maine. Some girls rave about the natural rock deodorant.

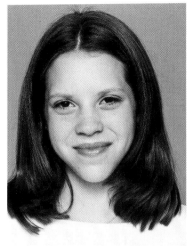

Before: I love Lisa's cute girly look.

After: But...for when she wants that grown-up look...I evened out Lisa's skin, defined her eyes with mascara, used a little blush, and a full-on (glamorous but still natural) lip color.

Before: Best friends Chloe and Nefertiti couldn't be happier.

After: We played with fun shadows (brown color on Nefertiti and shimmery white on Chloe), evened out skin tone (with concealer), and did pretty lips. Now they just need somewhere fun to go!

You can never be positive you won't get a bad haircut. I've been there myself and have had lots of disappointing cuts. It's smart to start with the smallest of trims—you can always cut more later. Hair stylists love to cut hair—that's what they've trained to do. If you go into a salon asking for something new, chances are the stylist will cut a lot of your hair off. It's smart to go into a salon knowing exactly what you want. If you don't know (and it sounds like you don't yet know), go see a stylist for a consultation. Talk through your options. Take along pictures of a look that you like. Then leave, go home, talk to your friends and mom about it before you take any big dramatic actions. It's pretty horrible when you get a bad cut. You feel like it's the end of the world. And—no matter what anyone says—it is. At least for a day or two.

In the case of a **bad haircut**, buy some cute barrettes, headbands, and clips, and experiment with different styles. Slick back short hair. If it's long enough to pull back, do a ponytail (*for more ideas, see chapter 26, Hair).*

Left: No makeup is the right look for Taylor, 11. She is beautiful as she is.

I think drinking lots of water and eating fresh foods helps your skin. A good cleansing plan also makes a difference. Once you notice acne, see a dermatologist. There are lots of ways to treat acne today. You might get your sister some help, as well.

Preteen Skin Care

1. Wash your face morning and night with a gentle soap. Rinse soap off with fifteen splashes or more.

2. Use blemish products if you need them.

3. Apply a liquid moisturizer on your face if it feels tight after you wash it. If you have extremely oily skin, use an oil-control lotion, instead.

Makeup for twelves

• sheer shimmer shadows
• sheer lip colors and glosses
• the wildest, strangest nail colors you can find!

Don't obsess over your weight. Just be smart about watching your diet and making sure you get lots of good exercise. Some people simply have slower metabolisms than others. If that's the case with you, you'll need to put a lot of energy into your body (*see chapter 12).* And remember: There's no guarantee that you'll get your mom's body— maybe you've got your dad's body genes!

15 GO FOR IT: EXPERIMENTAL MAKEUP

Sticking to the same safe, natural makeup can get boring. Or old. This chapter explains some creative ways to show your personality with makeup and still look pretty. The important thing to remember with experimental color: Try everything first in the safety of your own home at a moment when you've got plenty of time to flub up and start over.

Or, go to a beauty counter and try something absolutely new. What's the worst thing that could happen? You hate it and have to wash your face!

Only if you L-O-V-E the results, feel comfortable in the look, and run it by your best friend(s) with over-whelmingly positive results, should you go out.

WEAR IT…DON'T LET MAKEUP WEAR YOU.

Indre For a disco-party night or costume-party look…try a little face jewelry like this ruby teardrop. I made the lips shiny red just for fun.

Alison Cutts Green see-through shadow: a fun way to play with color, but still in a natural, soft way. Tame enough for school days.

Here's **Monique**, soft and natural—peachy eyes, soft cheeks, and glossy lips. I did a matte turquoise shadow for a big statement eye. But the look is still fresh because I didn't pile on lots of mascara or

liner. The lip is kept quiet, too, with just a little gloss. Eyes always come across more serious.

Saskia So…your hair is red and everyone has always told you not to wear a red lip. With the right blue-red lip color (avoid orangey reds) see how amazing it looks. If your skin is pale and you find that magic red lipstick (buy several tubes), why not make it your signature accessory. It's a great party look.

Hana Hettesova Here I used foundation on her lips to make them as pale as possible and did a smoky, dark eye. I used matte Royal Blue shadow thick on her lid—which sets off her chestnut eyes. Not your average 8 AM English lit look…(i.e., save this one for Saturday night).

Green/blue nail Why not go a little crazy with nail polish? Metallic colors, like this blue and green, have great shine, are cheap to buy and fun to wear. Just keep plenty of remover around for when you are ready to move on to pastels. And remember: What looks good on your hands late at night might not seem so great rushing off to school the next morning. You can get away with so much more on your toes. Red is my favorite choice for summer. It's a mistake-proof classic. But there are so many outrageous shades and finishes to choose from…

Allison Cutts It sounds stranger than it looks: Lavender eye shadow. But lots of unexpected colors can look really pretty. Find a favorite off-beat shade (don't spend a lot of money here), use your finger to spread it across your lid (don't worry if it's not perfect—in fact, it's better if it's a little rough), and head out the door. Don't obsess. With eyes like this, stick to a simple glossy lip.

Indre I love a fun lip color like this bubblegum pink one. The shine makes it modern (too matte or frosted wouldn't be as fresh). And keeping the rest of the face clean makes it young and cool.

WAYS TO PLAY

- **Color**: don't be shy. The easiest way to experiment is with color—you can go brighter, bolder, or pastel.

- You can also play with **texture**—try sheer color, the easiest to wear and the most flub-proof. Try matte for a sophisticated look or shimmer for a little excitement.

- Pick one feature at a time and go for it. Do your eyes really dramatic and smoky, or with a bright funky color shadow.

- **Lips** and **nails** are the low-commitment areas of makeup adventure. Wear a color you'd never, **ever** consider on your fingernails for a day. Do it as a **dare**…why not. You may find you love it.

16 SWEET 16 BEAUTY BASH
A PARTY GIRL'S DIARY

By Rebecca Plofker (Bobbi's niece)

Event: My Sweet 16 Party

Scene: Aunt Bobbi's house, one summer afternoon

The Girls:

Melissa Rassas: My incredibly animated friend who told me after the party, "That was the highlight of my life; it's downhill from here!"

Jackie Krupa: "Becca, we have to do this again before prom," Jackie told me, two, three, four, or five times during the party.

Rachel Wilkin: I have never received a thank-you note or call for having a party. Rachel's thank-you note might have been the first in history.

Ellen Munn: It's amazing, Ellen may have actually found a new favorite lip gloss!!!!

Nikki Fitzmaurice: With her new look, Nikki could finally stop complaining about her red skin. Her smile was even brighter; and her great laugh, well that could never change.

Beverly Bolton: Bev finally found makeup that she can wear in the real world, not only onstage.

Adrienne Thal: Even a makeup pro like Adee can pick up some new makeup tricks.

Laura Warshauer: Bobbi's makeup only added to Laura's shine.

Carey Felgendreger: My lunchtime buddy for the last two years, Carey is as nice on the inside as she looked on the outside.

Katie Vernon: One of the only ones who wears sunblock every day without Bobbi telling us to (because her mom makes her), Katie was smart to bring a raincoat—so the rain didn't smear her beautiful face!

Serena Shulman: If anyone would know the true power of Bobbi's make-up, it's Serena, who's so into my aunt that she did everything but stalk her.

Jessica Drewitz: She's my cousin who always looks pretty in pastels and always manages to get lots of Aunt Bobbi's makeup to play with.

Becca Plofker: ME! I am so lucky to have Bobbi Plofker as my aunt, not only because she is a makeup diva, but also she is such a cool person.

THE PARTY

To me she is my wonderful aunt Bobbi, but to my friends she was the master of makeup, Bobbi Brown. Greeted in her kitchen by Bobbi and her assistants (who at first we all thought were models because they are so gorgeous), we soon turned the house into a makeup studio.

We were a little self-conscious as we settled ourselves around Bobbi's big, wooden, dining room table. But, being teenage girls surrounded by one another, as well as piled-high plates of snacks, it wasn't long before we began doing what we do best, talking and pigging out.

SKIN CARE

Bobbi gave us some tips on how to keep our skin looking good and our faces zit-free. In talking with Bobbi, we decided that our major skin problems are zits, oiliness, and zits! We then talked about solutions.

There are so many products out there that promise to solve the oilies. It gets confusing. Bobbi helped us sort out the options. She told us that what we should be using is an oil-control moisturizer only on facial areas that are oily. (For me and my friends, that means our noses and foreheads.)

A SMALL PIMPLE SEEMS LIKE A BASEBALL WHEN WE LOOK IN THE MIRROR, AND WE ALL WANT TO KNOW HOW TO SUCCESSFULLY COVER IT UP.

How to successfully cover up a pimple is some-thing we all wanted to know. It seems that the biggest mistake we make is using products, like concealer, that dry up pimples, only making matters worse. Concealer also is too thick, drawing attention to our pimples. Bobbi explained that when the skin gets too dry it can't "breathe," trapping everything under the surface. Instead, we should be using cream foundation to cover our zits. Also, wearing moisturizer every day will help to prevent a breakout. Foundation works well only if you can't see it. Before using it, we have to remember to make sure that the color blends in well with our skin tone. (That seems like the hardest part.)

Healthy eating, getting lots of sleep, drinking tons of water, being happy, and not smoking are the best things that people can do for their skin. I knew that smoking was terrible for my body, but I didn't realize how quickly it could destroy skin. Bobbi has seen beautiful models who have lost their glow after smoking for a few years. Although we don't think about it now, we need to start pre-venting skin cancer before it's too late. I was really surprised that only three out of the thirteen of us wore sunblock daily. Bobbi advised us to wear SPF 15 every day.

MAKEUP

Bobbi went through everything for us, with great demonstrations. It's amazing that all the little things we were doing wrong make such a huge difference.

I agree 100 percent with Bobbi's belief that makeup is supposed to look natural and enhance the beauty that is already there.

For starters, some of us have freckles and Bobbi told us not to hide them. When putting on blush, Bobbi said that we should end up looking like we do after playing sports or exercising, with a healthy red glow in our cheeks. For eye shadow, the light colors should be on top, near the eyebrow, while the darker colors should be on the bottom. However, we don't need to wear very dark colors because we'd end up looking like something closer to Dracula's bride than a beauty queen! This is because dark colors are meant for older women. Most of us just like to wear lip gloss every day. Bobbi gave us a great suggestion—that we use a lip pencil to cover the lip after applying the lip gloss. The waxiness of the lip pencil ensures long-lasting lip shine. The two also combined create a great effect!

EYEBROWS

Although most teens (including me) tweeze our eyebrows, Bobbi is a strong believer that we shouldn't, because most teens overtweeze. Big problem, because eyebrows won't grow all the way back. So as long as it's to prevent a unibrow or get a few way-out-of-place hairs, eyebrow tweezing is okay. To shape our eyebrows, we can resort to makeup. Applying an eye shadow color, which is the same as our hair, with an eyebrow brush, we can create any shape without using tweezers.

AFTERMATH

After we were turned into beauty queens, we settled on the porch and dived into our pizza and salad. Looking around, I realized that the best part of Bobbi's makeovers was that everyone looked like herself. The makeup just brought out our strong characteristics and enhanced what was already there.

The best birthday party ever would not have been complete without a cake and a wish. The cake was decorated with (what else?) makeup, and written in my favorite colors, blue and yellow, was "Becca's 16th." In one breath I was able to blow out all 16 candles. My wish? Well…that's my secret. We went home glowing, with the **best** goody bags: products from Bobbi's own makeup line.

17 BRACES

THEY'RE NOT FOREVER

We cornered my local orthodontist, Edward D. Gold, D.D.S., to get the latest on braces. Here's what we heard:

The Score: Braces are a luxury. Most children on this planet won't ever have the opportunity to have braces, so consider yourself lucky to get them if you need them.

In Other Words: Don't complain. Be grateful to your folks for funding this expense. (A simple thank-you will do sometime in the next two to three years.) Wearing them now is better than having buck teeth the rest of your life or having to endure braces as an adult (which is more painful and takes longer).

Why: Braces are there first and foremost to help you keep your teeth healthy for the rest of your life. And, second, they're there to make your teeth their straightest and your smile its prettiest. (Who doesn't L-O-V-E a nice smile!?)

Rebecca Plofker: Here I kept the focus on the eyes by playing up her naturally strong brow. Then we had fun with some shiny lavender shadow on the lid. The mouth? Pale pink gloss. My favorite is her big sweet grin.

When to Take Action: Earlier is better. Some problems can be addressed as early as the age of seven. Most braces go on between twelve and fourteen.

Your Role: A teenager is old enough to take some responsibility for her body. If something about your teeth bothers you, ask your dentist if you need to see an orthodontist. Discuss with your parents and then plan a visit. Make sure you communicate any of your own concerns (teeth things you don't like, etc.) with your orthodontist. Don't feel like this is someone else's problem.

How to Get Them Off as Soon as Possible: Follow the rules. That means taking good care of your braces by brushing and flossing. You also must be careful not to break the braces or bend your wires. So be smart and avoid:

• Hard foods like ice, popcorn, pizza crust, fingernails, pencils, pen caps, etc. (This might be a good way to eliminate a not-so-pretty habit.)

• Sticky, gooey foods like bubble gum, caramel, taffy, corn on the cob.

When You've Had Enough: Ask your orthodontist

BRACES MAKEUP: FOCUS ON YOUR EYES AND KEEP YOUR MOUTH SIMPLE.

Installation: It's no big deal. A lot of kids get braces in the morning and then want to get back to school that day to show all their friends. If you are apprehensive, plan on a summer day or Friday PM appointment.

How Long You'll Wear Them: For the most minor of corrections, expect six to eight months. The average amount of time spent in braces is two and a half years. If your correction is serious, it could even be longer. Then, after the big hardware is off, plan on wearing a retainer full-time for eight to twelve months and after that just at night.

The Surprising Thing: A lot of kids think braces are really cool. Sometimes it seems more kids have them than not! I had them for three and a half years!

if you can see the model of your mouth and pictures of your teeth. He'll explain the progress you have made and show you what's left. Chances are, you'll be convinced to stick it out. Once they're off, the long painful process will fade away fast.

What They Can Do For You: Besides promising a most beautiful smile that you'll appreciate for the rest of your life, braces can actually change the look of your face. If your teeth crowd together and jut out, braces will bring them back in line, making your mouth look less prominent and more in balance with the rest of your face. If, on the

Jessica: I applied pastel shadow, a little liner, and black mascara on her eyes. Pale pink blush brings out Jessica's awesome cheeks.

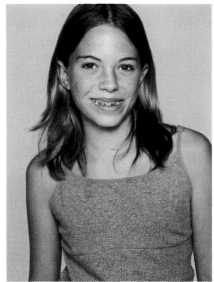

Chloe Silber, 12

Self-conscious about: Braces, even though "I know they're helping my teeth."

Bobbi's advice: Switch the focus to the eye with pale or shimmery shadow, and use only clear gloss (anything red or pink will draw attention to the braces) on the mouth.

Aftereffect: "I thought braces would change my look, but they don't have to." A good thing, too, since Chloe has 16 months left, and counting.

other hand, your teeth are too far back in your mouth, braces can help fix an empty or hollowed-out look to the mouth.

HANG-UPS TO GET OVER:

1. **THAT THEY'LL MAKE YOU UGLY.**
2. **THAT THEY'LL RUIN YOUR SOCIAL LIFE.**
3. **THAT NO BOY WILL EVER KISS YOU IN BRACES.**

MAKEUP OPTIONS

GLOSS AND BRACES GO WELL TOGETHER SINCE BRACES TEND TO DRY OUT YOUR LIPS.

This might be your time to play up your eyes—draw attention away from your mouth if it bugs you. Or…break the rules and go for it wearing a bright lip color or matching your lipstick to your mouth bands.

Role Models

Niki Taylor became an overnight success when she burst on the scene at the age of fifteen. And I remember well her mouthful of silver braces. That didn't stop her from launching one of the biggest careers in the history of modeling!

Bobbi's braces: I wore them for three and a half years—almost my entire time in high school. And…yes…I did have a boyfriend the entire time. I, like everyone, hated them at first and had to adjust. But I, like you, got used to them. I just kept telling myself: They are helping my teeth and my beauty and my smile—things I will have for the rest of my life!

DECORATING OPTIONS

Braces are available in:

- Silver: the classic look that most kids choose
- Clear: you hardly can see that they're there!
- Gold plate: for those who just want to flaunt it!

Ligatures The ties that attach wires to braces and that are changed every four to six weeks offer some cool accessorizing possibilities since they come in a million colors like…neon…orange and black for Halloween….red and green for Christmas… your school colors…pastels…glow-in-the-dark shades…teal…and more!

At the very least, these bands might give you some sense of control over your mouth.

Braces Big Sister

Find a braces big sister—someone who's been there. Ask her what the worst times were and how to prepare yourself. Ask her for comfort tips and eating ideas, too. There are **no stupid questions**. If you don't know anyone, ask your orthodontist to connect you with a patient who's been through it.

Before you know it, you'll be doing the favor for someone younger.

18 AFRICAN AMERICAN TEEN BEAUTY

I hate to generalize about girls, but I see it all the time: White girls obsess about their bodies and black girls obsess about their hair. My advice is to stay simple and don't fight the "Hair God." I love a ponytail slicked back—this is a great option for those of you who have a "hair thing." Hair extentions are a much bigger commitment but can be amazing. Either way, just be who you are. The best you can be. Choose a beauty role model whom you adore (there are **a lot** to choose from) and give your makeup and skin care a little attention, too.

PRETTY, SIMPLE MAKEUP: STEP BY STEP

1. Start with clean bare skin. Apply the right moisturizer for your skin type, and allow a few seconds for it to absorb (see *Biggest Issue: Your Skin, page 108)*.

2. Apply concealer (make sure it is yellow-toned— not orange, not pink, not red, and one to two shades lighter than your skin tone) to any under-eye circles or blotchy patches.

3. Do your personal foundation number (*see Foundation Basics, page 108*) or skip this step if concealer alone gives you even skin tone. (Note: It's not uncommon for some dark skin to require three different shades to even out skin tone.)

Naye goes from bare and beautiful to polished and pretty.

4. Set your face with tinted powder.

5. Fill your brow in with dark brown shadow. Do it a little stronger than you'd like, then soften with a powder puff.

6. Apply liner to top lid.

7. Apply blush to the apples of your cheeks.

8. Do neutral lip color for day. Or…a blackberry or red lip for night.

Biggest Issue: Your Skin

The key to looking your best is smooth, even-toned skin. If your skin is oily, you risk looking greasy. If it is dry, your skin can take on an ashy appearance. The right moisturizer can handle both of these problems. Shop around and experiment. It's smart to take your time and spend a little extra cash (if necessary) to find one that really works for you.

Oily Skin: Find an **oil control** or **shine control** lotion. Smooth it on only the oily parts of your face. Use an oil-free moisturizer at night or on dry spots during the day.

Dry Skin: Find a moisturizing lotion.

Really Dry Skin: Use a moisturizing cream or even an **oil** made for the face.

• Be aware that keloid skin scars very easily. Black skin tends to be nice and thick, but marks from blemishes or too much picking are quite noticcablc. Try putting vitamin E on spots to help them heal. Cocoa butter is a great moisturizer to have on hand.

FOUNDATION BASICS

A lot of black women need three different colors of foundation to balance out the darkest and lightest zones of their faces. This sort of blending is a really advanced makeup technique, so don't be discouraged if you don't get it right away. I often find black women to be some of the most talented makeup artists around because they've had to figure out a way to even out the tones on their own faces. Many famous actresses and models I've worked with have this problem.

Start here: With a clean, un-madeup face, stand in front of a mirror in a room where there is some natural light from a window. Try to distinguish the different zones of your face. Is your face all the exact same color? (If so, you are really lucky. But chances are, you've probably got a few different colored zones going on.) Where is your face its darkest? (Check out under your eyes.) Where is it lightest? (Most likely your cheeks are the lightest area of your face.) What zone is somewhere in between? (Probably your forehead.)

Light: Apply under eyes—on darkest portion of skin.
Medium: Wear on your forehead to balance the other zones.

Dark: Apply on cheeks—on lightest zone of your face.

DON'T BOTHER

I love experimentation. But my years as a makeup artist have taught me that there are some things black women shouldn't even bother trying…

SKIP THIS,
BECAUSE OF THIS

- Light-colored foundation to try to lighten skin
  Because…It looks horrible
- Foundation with SPF that contains zinc oxide
  Because…Your skin will look ashy
- Translucent powder
  Because…Your skin will look pasty

YOUR PERFECT MAKEUP KIT

- **Concealer**—Find a yellow-toned product that is one shade lighter than skin tone.
- **Foundation**—You'll need two, possibly three shades if your skin tone is darker on your forehead, for example.
  One matches skin tone exactly.
  One is one shade darker than skin tone.
  One is one shade lighter than skin tone.
- **Powder**—Find a tinted powder (loose or pressed) that is yellow- or orange- toned. (**Exception**: Girls with very dark complexions should find a powder with a blue tint.)
- **Brow filler**—Find a shadow that's the same color as your hair. Dark brown shadow that has no red in it and isn't ashy is a good bet. Don't use black

on your brows (it's too harsh and unnatural).
Reddish browns are good for hair that has had
a henna treatment.

Go lighter, like sable, if your hair is bleached.

- Shimmery Eye Shadow—For when you want
  to do something special. Filled-in brows and
  black mascara may be all that you need!
- Black Mascara—I love using black. It gives a
  strong eye and makes the eye pop without
  looking too made up.
- Pink and/or Plum Blush
- Pink and Blackberry Lipsticks

Must-have tools:

- Tweezers
- Brow brush

The Girls Who Get It Right: Beauty Role Models

These young women aren't afraid to show their own distinct personalities with their looks. They have developed their own personal beauty styles and are an inspiration to the rest of us.

Brandy

Aaliyah

Venus Williams

Serena Williams

Jada Pinkett Smith

Lauryn Hill

Queen Latifah

P.S. HAIR

It's important that—whatever style you choose—your hair is well conditioned. Short, short hair is easy and cool-looking. Hair extensions are another amazing option. Some girls want to try chemically straightening their hair, but I'd explore all your other possibilities first.

PRETTY IN PINK

Don't be afraid of **soft colors** that your blond friends wear all the time. In this photo, I did the same exact light shimmery makeup on both Jen (right) and Naye (left). Pale pink works beautifully on a dark lip: All you need to do is line the lip with a slightly darker pencil, then blend it carefully with the pink.

19 LATIN AMERICAN TEEN BEAUTY

The Latin women I know have such incredible natural beauty. They have amazing skin and hair color. Most of these women seem to appreciate their femininity and sexiness. I can honestly say that they seem more comfortable with their bodies than lots of other women I know, and have more fun flaunting it.

Yet I find many Latin girls wear too much makeup and simply don't need it. My message? Let your natural beauty show! Experiment with sexy, wearable shades—on you, quieter colors are sexy; loud fuchsia is not!

Skin Notes

Keep your skin clean and don't pick! Darker skin tones scar more easily. Sunscreen is important even if you tan easily—no one looks good in dark, prune-y skin!

Hair Help

Avoid funky cuts and color. Go with your natural resource: thick shiny hair! Keep it healthy and strong. Wear it to your shoulders or longer. In your case, more is better!

COLORS COUNT (A LOT!)

Things to Avoid and What Works

Since many Latin girls have a beautifully rich skin

tone, the colors you choose to wear on your face come across really strongly. That's why you need to be an expert in discerning warm, deep colors that complement your beauty from the overly bright colors that will look brash or harsh. Remember: What's cute in a magazine doesn't always work in real life.

Instead of Fuchsia Lips
Do Plum Lips

Instead of Red or Hot Pink Lips
Do Rose or Raspberry Lips

Instead of Coral Lips
Do Honey Lips

Instead of Orange Lips
Do Bronze Lips

Instead of Turquoise or Emerald Shadow
Do Gold Shimmer

Instead of White Shadow
Do Banana or Taupe

If, instead, you are pale with blond or red hair, look for colors and role models that suit your look. More Gwyneth Paltrow and less Jennifer Lopez.

Three Key Tips

Foundation: It's very, very important that you find a product with a yellow-gold undertone to match the warmth of your natural skin tone.

Powder: Also needs to be golden in color.

Lip Liner: It shouldn't be noticeable. Lining your lip with a darker color than your lipstick is old-fashioned and not pretty. Try a light lipstick and a deep (not dark!) lip pencil. Blend well!

ALWAYS REMEMBER:

Don't overdo it…A beauty like yours doesn't need much help. It's easy to look sexy. But go a little heavy, and you push your look over-the-top.

The Goal: To look sexy, simple, and classic.

Beauty Role Models

Jennifer Lopez

Salma Hayek

Gloria Estefan

Daisy Fuentes

20 ASIAN AMERICAN TEEN BEAUTY

The young Asian women I know have no idea how beautiful they are. This is amazing to me, since I think they are some of the most gorgeous teenagers on this planet! Part of the problem is what all of us face: a low self-esteem. But the other part of the problem is that there are so few visible Asian female role models for young Asian women to look up to: Asian women are horribly under-represented in the worlds of advertising, modeling, and even in Hollywood. It drives me crazy that even in Japan, Caucasian models or only part Asian girls are preferred over Japanese girls in advertising and magazines. This makes no sense to me: Asian girls need Asian role models...Hopefully that's a situation we will all work to change. But, in the meantime, just remember that your own beauty is spectacular. Try to appreciate your own features and don't try to be someone you're not!

Eyebrows: You'll want to get good at filling in your brow. (Your eyebrows may have short, coarse hairs.) Buy an eyebrow brush and a brown shadow and **practice**. Well-defined brows will really enhance your beautiful face and bring strength to your eyes.

Eyes: The biggest mistake? Going dark and dramatic. Avoid contouring with black shadow because that will make your eyes look small and more recessed (which is probably one of your complaints with yourself anyhow). Instead, use a lighter shadow all over your eyelid and a medium tone shadow for a soft contour.

Lining your eyes is the next most important thing after filling in your brows. Use a brush and a deep shadow. Line all the way around your eye. Check that it is thick enough on top to see when you open your eyes.

Cheeks: Don't attempt to sculpt your cheeks with complicated contouring techniques. By the same token, don't skip this step in your makeup routine! A simple pink blush on your cheeks will make you look pretty.

Lips: Most Asian girls have the most gorgeous full lips. You can wear anything!!! Go for sheer gloss or full-on red lipstick, and you'll probably look amazing. Have fun experimenting with color.

Hair: Keep the cut simple and the texture straight. Whatever you do: **Don't ever even consider getting a perm!**

THE PERFECT MAKEUP KIT

- Concealer/foundation—Yellow-toned
- Matte brown shadow—To fill in brow
- Thickening black mascara
- Three eye shadows
    1. one that's soft, for all-over color on lid
    2. a second that's medium, for lid contour
    3. and a third that's dark, to use in lining eyes

- **Pink blush** (cream or powder)
- **Lips** Go for it!!! Have a whole lip collection from subtle to crazy.

Must-Have Tools
- **Tweezers**
- **Baby scissors** (to trim too-long brow hairs)
- **Eyebrow brush** (a hard one, with slanted bristles)

AVOID AT ALL COSTS

Two things I think you can live without
Skin-whitening cream—I see this when I travel in Asia and I don't like it. Instead, enjoy your own natural skin color—it's perfect the way it is!
Pink foundation—It'll make you look like a doll—totally artificial.

Before: No makeup—pretty.

After: With makeup—stunning! Foundation, blush, smoke eyes, and soft pink lip.

TOTALLY SAFE MAKEUP LOOK

What could be more classic…you can't go wrong with this!
Simple liner, berry or pink lips

TWO MORE EDGY LOOKS

Dark Eyes
Smoky eyes (still stay close to lashes with shadow)
Pastel blush, pale lip color
Strong Mouth-Red or wine matte or glossy lip.
That's all you need to be glam-gorgeous!

21 GLOBAL BEAUTY

So…your father is African American and your mother Vietnamese American. What does that make you?

GLOBAL BEAUTY IS A MOST MODERN CATEGORY OF GORGEOUS GOOD LOOKS.

Decades ago you actually needed to have blond hair and blue eyes to be considered to be a model…now it's actually hard to find models who look the part of an old-fashioned "all-American" girl. The blond hair and blue eyes popular in the '60s are now considered slightly boring in the beauty world, while cross-cultural combinations like green eyes with dark, dark skin or corksckrew black hair with pale, pale ivory skin are embraced as more exciting and interesting.

You get the picture—global beauty is major. Plus, since the world is getting smaller and smaller (you're only as far away as your cell phone), global looks is the wave of the future. Hopefully you'll find yourself here in the pictures. But remember, no one…..**no one** looks exactly like you. And your uniqueness is something to celebrate!

But we all want practical help and that's where a global girl needs to be extra smart. You'll need to pick and choose beauty information from all the chapters that apply. There is no formula for you: Think of yourself as a **work of art**!!!

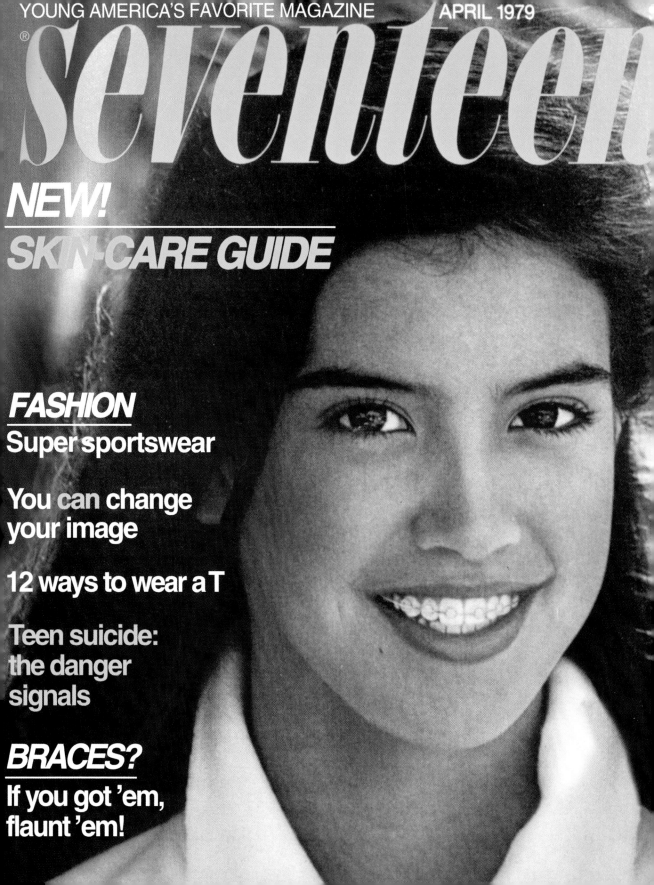

YOUNG AMERICA'S FAVORITE MAGAZINE   **APRIL 1979**

seventeen

NEW!
SKIN-CARE GUIDE

FASHION
Super sportswear

You can change your image

12 ways to wear a T

Teen suicide: the danger signals

BRACES?
If you got 'em, flaunt 'em!

22 TEEN YEARBOOK

Yes, it's tough being a teenager. For most of us, it's one of the roughest times of our lives. And if you think you're all alone, think again.

Do you look at other girls and assume they are perfect? That they have always been that way? Pretty, happy, confident, and comfortable with their bodies? Well...the truth is, they probably have the same insecurities you do.... They spend just as much time obsessing over stuff they can't stand.

Role models. We create our own. And sometimes we just don't get what's going on inside their heads. And, to prove my point, we've asked some well-known women how they felt as teens. When you check out what some of the world's most visible, successful, and beautiful women have to say about their lives as teens, it sounds pretty familiar!

Phoebe Cates, Actress

When I was fifteen, I thought my hair was too straight, my teeth not straight enough, my coloring too dark, and my bottom lip too big. I wanted to be the look that was "in." Think Farrah Fawcett. No one was more surprised than I to wind up on the cover of *Seventeen* magazine, braces and all. (I learned that the look that is "out" can also be "in.") Even after the cover came out, and because I was a teenager, I **still** thought my hair was too straight, my teeth not straight enough, my coloring too dark, and my bottom lip too big. Being a teenager is hard

From left to right: Geena Davis, Whitney Houston, Christie Brinkley, Marlee Matlin, Oprah Winfrey, and Sarah McLachlan

for everyone. My advice? Have compassion (especially for yourself) and stick together. You're all in the same hormonal boat.

Marlee Matlin, Actress

Being a teenager was all about testing my limits. Sometimes it came with good results, and sometimes it came with bad. I remember very clearly calling home to tell my parents I wasn't going to make it home in time for my curfew. "Dad…I'm out of gas," or "Dad, I'm lost and don't know where I am right now." Most kids would expect that their parents would yell at them and tell them that this kind of game doesn't work. But, seeing as I was able to speak to them and not hear them because I'm deaf, I took full advantage of playing it both ways.

A lot of times it worked. I could stay out for hours after my curfew and play innocent when I came home. But one time it didn't work. My parents called the cops, and I remember being very surprised when I realized my parents had stopped letting me get away with taking advantage of my deafness.

Every teenager seems to want to make waves in order to find out who they are. I know—I've been there. If you asked me now, "Would you have done things differently?" I probably would say yes. But that's because I'm a mother now and worry about my daughter in the same way that my parents probably did about me. But I also know that growing up means you have to go through the hard times in order to learn your lessons. Far be it for any of us to deny you the experience of growing up.

But at nineteen, I learned a very important lesson. It was never to give up your dreams, even if fast cars and parties and friends seem more important. If I had not listened to my heart and pursued what I was really good at, acting, when I was nineteen, I would have never starred in *Children of a Lesser God*, and won an Academy Award when I was twenty-one.

Martha Stewart, lifestyle guru

There are only a few things I would be presumptuous enough to tell a young girl living in today's complicated world:

Study very, very hard.

Stand up very, very straight.

Be as natural as you can possibly be.

Bobbi Brown, Beauty Queen

I never liked being five feet, zero inches. I wasn't always happy being a brunette and wished my hair had been straighter (that was the hippie look of my time). I didn't always love my eyes. Too not blue? Too deep set? But now, looking back, I realize that all those hang-ups drove me to be a makeup artist and to help others dealing with their same insecurities. Because I've been there, I can help others in the same situation.

Niki Taylor, model

Being a teen is the most difficult time in your life, both from a physical and an emotional view. No one understands you, and your hormones are bouncing off the wall.

Just remember from one who's been there, give it time and believe in yourself. Listen to good advice from those who care about you as well, because, although you might not like hearing it, they are telling you the whole truth and nothing but the truth!

Opposite: Gwyneth Paltrow, Sheryl Crow, Mary Tyler Moore, Rosie O'Donnell, Rene Russo, Madonna Ciccone, Katie Couric, Diane Sawyer, Michelle Pfeiffer.

23 TEEN BEAUTY TODAY

WHAT GIRLS LIKE/WHAT GUYS LIKE

TEEN BEAUTY PROFILE

To make sure we addressed all your possible teenage beauty issues in this book, we asked the girls we know all about their habits and complaints. What did we learn?

- Young women today are a lot hipper than any generation before.
- Teenagers today are really smart about both sun protection (a lot wiser than I was!) and skin care.
- And, not surprisingly, today's girls have really strong opinions about what they like and don't.
- The best thing we discovered? There is no right answer—diversity reigns with this generation. Below, some of what we found out.

Celebrities whose beauty cabinet girls would most like to raid?

Hands-down favorite:

Gwyneth Paltrow's—"because she always looks beautiful, but never too done"

Can't help adoring:

Drew Barrymore's—"because we love her bright lipstick and glitter"

Other beauty idols: Jennifer Aniston, Courteney Cox Arquette, Cameron Diaz, Calista Flockhart

Washes face: Twice daily

Biggest Beauty Complaints
(in order of importance):

1. Zits
2. Shiny skin
3. Bushy brows

Favorite At-Home Treatments
Peel-Off Masks (because they're fun)

Things about themselves they hate:
Forehead, feet, butt, hair, thighs, pimples, teeth, lips, eyes, belly button….(You name it—someone hates it!)

Feature girls like most about themselves:
Eyes

Favorite feature to play up:
Most said: **eyes**
A lot said: **skin**

If stranded on a desert island, couldn't live without:
Most girls said: Sunscreen (smart!!!!)
A lot said: Lip gloss
Only a few said: Mascara

First Time to Wear Makeup:
Most said: Age 13

The professional beauty treatment she'd most like to have?
Most girls said: Massage
Some said: Facial

A few said manicure and pedicure

How long does it take to do makeup every morning:
Some teenagers said **zero** time (i.e., they don't wear makeup every morning or do it at school or on the way to school). But most commit between 5 and 10 minutes to makeup every AM.

Scent?
Most young women love playing with scent and own between 3 to 6 fragrances.

Lipstick Like or Lipstick Love?
Half of the girls we asked own fewer than three lip colors, the other half own between ten and twenty.

The main motivator in buying a beauty product?
Color was the top answer. Ingredients and price tied for second.

Where you wear the MOST MAKEUP?
To parties. To dances.

Where you wear the LEAST MAKEUP?
To school. To church/temple. Anywhere my father is.

BOYS ON BEAUTY

What guys like. Really.

We conducted a completely anonymous survey of the teenage guys (ages 13 to 19). We asked them their feelings about girls' body type, hair, makeup look, and more. The reason we wanted to get at their preferences? **Not** so that you change your life or anything. But because information is power, and we thought you'd like to know.

Hairstyle boys like most on girls?

Long over short. (Some sensitive ones admitted that it depended on the girl. Duh!)

Do guys like makeup?

Yes—they are into makeup, and like when girls wear it…as long as it's not "too much" or "too obvious."

Is lip gloss a turn-on or turn-off?

Most boys like lip gloss (some admitted they liked the taste; others said they liked the way it made a girl's mouth look).

The ones who didn't like gloss (a minority) said they think it makes a girl look like she just ate "goo."

Favorite way to see a girl's lips?

Gloss—big winner

Natural—next big winner

Red lips—scored pretty high, too (but, do they really mean it??)

Feature a guy first notices?

A girl's eyes.

Favorite body type?

Most guys said tall and thin.

A lot of guys said not too skinny and not too fat.

Big beauty turn-off?

Finding "brown stuff" (foundation) on their clothes

Girl of their dreams?

Most guys said sexy and steamy

A lot of guys said soft and romantic

A few guys said down-to-earth and natural

A couple of guys said strong and athletic

(P.S. Then there were the guys who circled all four categories…)

Is watching a girl apply makeup a turn-on or turn-off?

No—most guys would rather not watch.

Would you feel deceived if you discovered that someone you liked (and thought was really natural) was actually wearing a lot of makeup?

A big fat **no**.

The bottom line: Guys don't have as many beauty hangups as we thought.

24 SO...YOU WANT TO BE A MODEL?

To most young women, modeling seems like an amazing career. You meet glamorous people, you travel to the coolest places, you make a ton of money, and all you have to do is look pretty....The truth is that modeling is not as glamorous as it looks. First of all, it's extremely hard to make it as a model. For every one hundred girls who step foot into the major American modeling agencies, only one will actually get signed by them. Even then, her chances of making it are slim...approximately only one model in ten thousand will be able to make it her career.

LET'S FACE IT...THERE ARE PROBABLY ONLY **TWENTY-FIVE SUPERMODELS** IN THE ENTIRE WORLD.

Modeling means long hours, lots of sitting around and waiting, and sometimes hard or uncomfortable work. (Just imagine trying to look happy wearing a bikini in the snow, and you get the picture.)

The basic requirements of modeling count most of us out. You have to be tall—five feet ten inches or taller. You have to be extremely thin. And, you have to be young—most girls start between the ages of thirteen and seventeen.

If you are determined to explore the possibilities, here's my step-by-step advice:

1. Get permission from your family—you will need their support and/or blessing.

2. Send a couple of simple snapshots to local agencies (see a listing in the back of this book). Do a full-length picture and a headshot. If you live anywhere near New York City, Miami, or Los Angeles, skip the local approach and write to agencies in these cities.

Important: Don't spend money hiring a local photographer—instead find a friend who's taking photography classes or someone else you know who is good with a camera.

Don't do tricky hair or makeup and don't wear anything too overpowering—keep everything **simple**!

3. Call agencies to schedule a "**go see**."

4. Go on the go see with clean hair and no makeup, and wear simple clothes and shoes you can walk in. (Most models going on go sees show up in cool jeans, tanks, and sneakers.) Be comfortable.

5. If one agency rejects you ("too small," "too pretty," "not right," etc.), go to two or three other agencies.

6. If you are "signed" to an agency, don't under any circumstances pay money for any of the following:
- test photo session (it's the agency's obligation)
- hair and makeup for photo session (ditto)
- putting together your portfolio (it's in the agency's

best interest for you to have the best book possible)

WHEN IT'S CLEARLY NOT WORKING

Switch gears—give modeling a shot locally, in your town. Or, make a big adjustment and try auditioning for commercials, take an acting class, explore doing makeup or styling. All of these are potential careers that would put you in the same environment. But most importantly **stay in school**—graduate.

The girls who make it big as models may not necessarily be the most beautiful girls in the world—they just photograph extremely well and have the audacity it takes to make it in this tough world. Many, many pretty girls are not right for modeling—but they are still beautiful.

Some better things to do with your life than model:
Go to the prom
Excel in sports
Have fun with your friends
Learn to play the guitar
Write a short story
Start taking pictures
Volunteer to help with your school yearbook
Get in touch with nature

WHAT GIRLS WHO'VE MADE IT HAVE TO SAY...

One day on the set of a photo shoot, I sat down

with three gorgeous teenage models I'd just made-up. They are from three very different places. They have three very different looks. They have all "made it," in the sense that they all are making a living modeling. These three young women seemed like a good source of advice for someone just starting out.

Korina, sixteen, from Croatia, has been modeling for 3 years. Her first job? Walking first down the runway at a Prada show in Milan. It was her first time in high heels and an incredible start.

Lisa Seiffert, seventeen, from Australia, began working as a model at age 12. She's been almost everywhere on jobs and still loves seeing new places. Keeping her eyes open this particular day was a challenge, though, since she'd just flown in from Sydney the night before.

Tia Holland, nineteen, from Florida, started out one year ago. She moved to New York City just after she graduated from high school. Her biggest booking yet? She'd just returned from the London runway shows. Her first time abroad.

Message to you:

Korina: Know that it's not an easy job.

Tia: It's really time-consuming and all-consuming.

Korina: You think you have a day off to rest and then you're on a plane to Asia.

Lisa: It's extremely hard to get where you want to be…to the level of modeling you dream of. Also, it takes a long time to make money. You can owe money to your agency for a long time.

Korina: That you can be the most beautiful girl in the world and not make it as a model. It takes the right personality.

Lisa: You have to really want this.

What you need to possess to succeed:

Tia: You need to be very passionate. You need to be very strong.

Korina: You have to be a strong personality or else you'll lose yourself trying to satisfy everyone else… your agent, the photographer, and the editors or client.

Tia: You need to be willing to stick it out and not let negative responses get you down. I had people tell me that I need a nose job. Or, that I needed to lighten my skin. That could have broken me down and sent me home together. But I stuck it out…

Lisa: You need to be relaxed about jet lag.

Korina: You need to just be yourself. Be natural.

Favorite modeling moment:

Tia: Doing the runway shows in London.

Korina: Doing John Galliano's show in Paris, where she was asked to play a part on the runway rather than just walk.

Lisa: Bali and every other exotic location she's visited.

What they want out of modeling:

Tia, Korina, Lisa: To be a supermodel. To make it in the way that Cindy Crawford, Stephanie Seymour, and Claudia Schiffer have.

25 SMELLING GOOD/ SMELLING BAD

WHAT YOU DON'T WANT TO WEAR?
YOUR MOTHER'S OLD STINKY PERFUME.

What smells good to you? Brownies in the oven? A newly cut lawn? Baby powder? Your dad's aftershave? The inside of a new car? You can start enjoying scent more just by being more aware of which ones give you a pleasurable feeling. Consider which ones irritate you: Mothballs? Kitty litter? Your brother's icky bedroom? Hot tar? Moldy cheese?

Sometimes the right scent can actually send you to a happy memory. Maybe a whiff of peonies makes you think of your grandmother in her flower garden. Finding that smell to wear on your skin just might re-create a good association. When I'm stressed, I wear Je Reviens because it reminds me of my aunt who is always calm.

The world of smells can be an exciting personal adventure. Just remember two things:

1. You don't have to smell like your mother or your grandmother. There are a lot of cool, young smells out there that aren't stinky and overpowering.

2. Don't let the stressful, overwhelming experience of buying a fragrance ruin it for you.

Start Simple

Buy one-note fragrances (like lavender or rose water). Or go to health food stores and buy essential oils. They cost around $8 each and are light and simple to wear. Here are some of my favorite essences and how they will make you feel:

Grapefruit or Orange: gives you energy

Ylang-ylang: a warm, balanced essence

Lemon: makes you feel clean

Patchuli: gives you a happy life

Peppermint: the caffeine of essences, it wakes you up

Lavender: relaxes you and helps you sleep

Eucalyptus: slightly medicinal-smelling and cleansing

Sandalwood: makes you feel warm and protected

Personal Scent Recipe:

Start with a base of apricot oil or safflower oil in a glass container. (You can use an empty fragrance bottle or vial that you've carefully cleaned.) Use the dropper from your essential oil bottle to add a few drops of the essential oils you most like. Add only a little at a time. Once you get a mixture you love, you can use it in lots of ways:

- Put it in unscented body moisturizer and smooth it all over your body after you shower.
- Put it in your conditioner for soft, pretty-smelling hair. It also works as a groomer!
- Put it straight on dry hair (rub a little oil on palms of hands and pat on hair) to stop fly away or static hair and to add shine.
- Put scented oil on your face in cold or dry weather (I know this sounds strange, but use just a little—it'll feel great and you won't break out).
- Make your own sachets by putting your scented oil on cotton balls; wrap the cotton in a piece of fabric and tie it up with a ribbon and put it in your closet or drawers.
- Put a drop of your oil on the lightbulb in your room for a pretty room scent.
- Keep a little in the shower to rub into your wet skin; Then pat skin dry with towel—skip moisturizer.

Other Cool Ways to Wear It—

Fragrance doesn't have to be applied the way they do in the movies-dabbed behind the ears and on the wrists. Find your own way to do it…wear it where it makes you most happy. A few of my favorite places:

1. I love it in your hair—what a cool way to wear scent: Spritz a cloud of scent in front of you and walk through it, letting the mist settle on your hair.

2. Put a tiny bit of a boyfriend's scent on the tip of your nose just to smell him for a while.

3. Wear scent all over your body by using scented body lotion or oil just after you shower.

4. The lightest possible way to wear scent? Use a scented shower gel. You're basically washing it off.

5. Two silly things to try: Scented nail polish or scented lip gloss.

THE BOTTOM LINE: DON'T FOLLOW RULES. WEAR ANYTHING THAT MAKES YOU FEEL GOOD!!

Seven Ways to Get Your Hands on Big Name Scents (without splurging)

1. Ask for samples—every major fragrance counter in department stores has boxes of those little glass vials. Don't be shy.

2. Go to the fragrance counter and spritz on a scent you're curious about. Look for the bottles labeled "**tester**"—that's what they're there for.

3. Check out scent strips in magazines.

4. Buy a mini bottle of scent. Look for in malls or in airports. It's a great way to try scents.

5. Nip a shot of a scent from a friend, friend's mom, your mom. Ask first—no one will say no.

6. Ask for a fragrance as a birthday, graduation, honor roll, or Christmas gift.

7. Check out the specials at discount drugstores.

Stuck with a Scent?

If you find yourself in the possession of a scent that you really don't love, what can you do? Leave the bottle open in your underwear drawer. (Be careful it doesn't tip. You can also put empty fragrance vials or bottles in drawers for a nice light scent.) Or let some friends try it—whoever loves it the most, gets it! Maybe they'll do the same for you.

Bobbi's Favorite First Scents

Must de Cartier (this one's really sexy)

Calvin Klein CK One (a cool unisex scent that's easy and light to wear)

Canoe (this was my first scent and yes, it's for men…why not?)

Chanel Cristal (this is one that'll grow with you…a take-away-to-College, easy-to-wear scent)

L'Air du Temps (sophisticated pretty—a brides-maid scent)

Lauren by Ralph Lauren (for the prepster lurking inside of each of us)

Love's Baby Soft (nonserious first scent—or for when you'd like to feel like a preteen again)

Jean Naté (noncommittal hot weather splash…for a sticky hot day)

The Gap scents (easy-going and calming—perfect for finals week)

W by Banana Republic (I like the soapy smell and the roll-on bottle. It fits well in my backpack.)

The Bottom Line: Don't follow rules. Wear anything that makes you feel good!!!

Going Against Type: I know this really cool girl named Amy who is into yoga, natural foods, hiking, environmental issues, and dogs. I was shocked when I learned she wears only Shalimar, a serious oriental scent from the '20s that her mother wears and her grandmother used to wear. (Amy loves how it reminds her of her family.) This made Amy seem even cooler to me. She's strong enough to wear it in her own laid-back way. And, somehow, on Amy, it comes across in a totally different way. **She wears the scent—she doesn't let the scent wear her**.

Big Fragrance Mistakes

THE BIGGEST MISTAKE? PUTTING ON TOO MUCH— START SMALL, ESPECIALLY IF YOU ARE EXPERIMENTING WITH A SERIOUS PERFUME.

How to wash it off? Change your clothes and take a shower.

Putting on several scents at the same time— **yuck**—this is a recipe for disaster.

Wearing your best friend's scent just because you like it on her.

Buying a fragrance on an impulse. Don't blow a lot of money unless you know it's the perfect thing. Unlike the last pair of black suede boots or the only size-7 skirt in the store that you love, the scent will still be there tomorrow.

Decoding the Language

Parfum: the strongest, richest, most expensive, longest-lasting way to wear scent—leave this to your mom or grandmom

Eau de Toilette or Cologne: diluted, lighter, contains more water—this is more for you

Splash, Mist, or Water: the lightest concentration—probably what you'll prefer

Essential oils: the pure elements of scents that you can buy at health food stores—they're cool and you control how much you wear.

MY DREAM SCENT: IT USED TO BE THAT WOMEN HAD ONE "SIGNATURE" SCENT THAT THEY'D ALWAYS WEAR. I THINK THAT'S OLD-FASHIONED AND BORING. MY "SIGNATURE" SCENT DOESN'T EXIST. I NEED TO HAVE A COLLECTION OF THEM. EVERY SIX MONTHS I FIND A NEW FAVORITE. I'M ALWAYS ON A SEARCH FOR MY DREAM SCENT.

BODY ODOR

Each of our bodies sends out smells. That's just the way we're built. But it's sometimes difficult to know whether our own personal body odor is overpowering or offensive to those around us. A morning shower is a good start for everyone. Regular washing of the hair is another.

Spritzing your body with scent isn't a substitute for a shower. It might change the smell of your body odor, but it won't cover it up entirely. Although, at the end of your day, if you have to go out directly from school, putting on a fresh-smelling scent may help you feel clean.

Deodorant vs. Antiperspirant
Deodorant takes away the body odor. Try to find a natural product that works for you at the health food store—those tall aerosol spray cans are nasty.

Antiperspirant helps limit or control the wetness under your arms. Again, a natural product would be my preference.
A light, first-step option is corn starch powder.

SMELLY FEET
I believe that foot odor comes from the inside. Maybe you're not drinking enough water or exercising enough. Think about treating it internally (check out a remedy at your health food store) and externally with corn starch powder.

BAD BREATH

You have bad breath. Yuck. If you are aware of it, chances are it's pretty intense. (It's hard to smell your own odors! Ask a family member to smell-check you, before you leave the house.) First, consider whether your mouth is really clean. Do you brush two or three times daily and floss nightly? Do you scrape your tongue to get debris off of it (you can buy a tongue scraper at a drugstore—you'll soon find yourself addicted!).

If your mouth is totally well maintained and clean, it could be that your stomach is "nervous" and produces extra acids that send up to your mouth bad-smelling juices. To correct, make sure you eat a balanced diet and that you eat often throughout the day. (If you're doing some crazy starvation diet like eating only green apples and broccoli, you might well have extremely bad breath.) Sugary mints don't work (believe me!). Chewing gum isn't really the answer either, since it can further stir up the acids in your system. The best solution is to get natural breath drops at a health food store.

DRINKING AND SMOKING ALMOST GUARANTEE THAT YOU'LL WALK AROUND WITH REALLY BAD BREATH. HOW COOL IS THAT?

26 HAIR—AN OWNER'S GUIDE

One big difference between you and your mom? She's probably settled on one basic hairstyle, while you probably like playing around with lots of different looks. And why shouldn't you? When you're a teenager, it's natural to want to experiment with your hair. Since I am an expert at makeup but not at hair (in fact, there are still moments when I am really confused about my hair!) I worked with Suzanna Romano, one of the top stylists in New York City, a partner in A.K.S. Salon on Madison Avenue, and a friend, to give you everything you need to know to get hair you love. Totally.

KNOWING YOUR HAIR

What's the cause of the biggest hair disasters? Going against your own natural hair texture. It's like when a girl with thick, curly hair decides to get a short blunt bob that would look great on her best friend who has straight hair. Look in the mirror and figure out what your hair texture is *(see the chart on the next page)*. There are a lot of things you can do to transform your hair look but **changing your hair texture isn't one of them**. Learn to like your hair texture. Get used to it. Live with it. It's part of you, and it's beautiful.

This is one of those basic lessons that I can say and save you lots of pain and suffering. But, then again, you might just have to get there on your

own, like I did. When I was in high school the "in" style was straight, thin, long hair. My friends and I used to iron our not-so-straight, not-so-thin hair. (Sounds strange, I know, but it's true.) Or, using two large, empty frozen OJ cans, we would set our hair on the top of our head and sleep like that. All of that for such a natural, hippie look...hmmm.

HAIR TEXTURE Straight and limp hair
ROLE MODEL Gwyneth Paltrow, Claire Danes, Calista Flockhart
PERFECT CUT bob or long and blunt

HAIR TEXTURE Curly or frizzy hair
ROLE MODEL Sarah Jessica Parker, Keri Russell, Andie MacDowell
PERFECT CUT Layers are key
Blunt cuts don't work

HAIR TEXTURE Thick and coarse hair
ROLE MODEL Julia Roberts, Lauryn Hill, Sandra Bullock
PERFECT CUT Vary lengths to take out bulk
Medium to long

HAIR TEXTURE Thick and Fine
ROLE MODEL Sarah Michelle Gellar
Nicole Kidman
PERFECT CUT All one length with layers around face (lots of hair volume but individual hairs are thin). Go very long (like hair most models have) or very short—growing out is painful.

ESSENTIAL HAIR EQUIPMENT

THE PRODUCTS

Shampoo Cream formula if you have dry hair. Clear formula for normal or oily hair.

Conditioner Rich formula for dry hair. Light formula for normal hair. Skip with oily hair.

Detangler Use in addition to conditioner for dry hair. Skip with normal hair. Use instead of conditioner for oily hair.

Treatment Hot oil hair mask for dry hair; clay hair mask for oily hair.

Optionals
  Gel
  Mousse
  Antifrizz spray or lotion

The word on styling products: Avoid using a lot of stuff in your hair. What's really pretty is simple, clean hair that has nice, natural movement. Don't use hairspray (too old-fashioned, except for fly-away help—*see page 161)*. For the best and most natural look, use styling products on **wet hair** only.

THE TOOLS

Wide-tooth comb—heavy-duty plastic

Flat-brush natural bristles are best. (A Mason Pearson brush is amazing and will last a lifetime, if you don't lose it!)

Round brush—avoid metal; again natural bristles are best.

Blow-dryer—find one with cool air option; the more powerful, the faster it will be. Don't throw away the nozzle—it helps you concentrate air on one area, which is what you need to do a good blowout.

Optionals
  Curling Iron
  Flattening Iron
  Crimping Iron

GETTING A GREAT CUT

• Ask around to find out the best salons in your community and who are the best stylists at those salons. Ask others with your particular hair type (i.e., corkscrew curls, superstraight) who does their hair. Have they had any hair disasters? Is there anyone to avoid?

• Be prepared to spend a little more than you might like.

• Decide what you want. Don't go to a stylist expecting that person to do something magical for you.

• Make sure you make yourself understood. Schedule a consultation with a stylist before you make the appointment for the cut. Take in pictures of how you want your hair to look. Ask whether

your ideas are realistic. Will the style you love work for your hair?

• If you are on the way to the sink to get your hair washed but you're not clear what is about to happen, **go back to the stylist and ask questions until you are clear about what is going to happen**. Don't be embarrassed—it's your hair!

• If you aren't great with a blow-dryer or don't have patience for it, specify that you want a "wash and wear" cut (i.e., no tricky blow-drying necessary).

HAIRCUT DISASTER

Everyone at the salon says how great the cut looks. You feel euphoric leaving the place. Your hair is shiny, bouncy, and beautiful. You feel like a new person. Then, the next morning, you wash your hair and you look like a squirrel. The hair just hangs there with no personality. How to prevent this scenario? Pay really close attention to the way the stylist is drying your hair.

But if you just can't re-create it at home, go back to the salon and ask for help. You may just need a really good blow-dry lesson. Make sure you are doing it yourself and not just watching someone else do it.

Ask whether your hair can be air dried…if so, what products should you use to get a look you like. Watch how the stylist uses the products….how much does he or she put on?

Ask for ideas on other styles that will work with the cut.

SORRY, I CAN'T. I HAVE TO WASH MY HAIR.*

Everyday washing is fine, especially if you do sports or have oily hair. Just be sure to create a diluted version of your shampoo so that you're not putting too much detergent on your hair. Most shampoos are just too strong for everyday use. Use an empty shampoo bottle or buy a bottle with a squeeze top. Fill the bottle halfway with your normal shampoo and fill the rest of the way with warm water. Use this diluted version to wash hair every other day.

Concentrate shampoo on the scalp—unless you use a lot of styling products, there's no need to shampoo ends of hair. Thorough rinsing will ensure that ends stay clean.

Rinse out shampoo really well…time yourself here and try to go for four minutes. A good rinse is just as important as a good wash in getting really clean hair.

WHEN TO COMB AND WHEN TO BRUSH
Comb wet hair in the morning after you shower. (**Brushing** wet hair can damage it.)

*This is a bad excuse. It's almost rude. Better to be honest and up front if you don't want to go out with the guy.

Brush dry hair at night before you go to bed. Your hair needs to be brushed, so make a habit out of it every evening. **Combing** dry hair is fine, too, but a brush will better distribute oils (i.e., make it shinier) and it's good for your scalp.

During the day carry a small brush around with you. If you invest in a natural-bristle brush (like a Mason Pearson one), leave it at home and don't risk losing it. Buy a nylon bristle one to keep in your locker or backpack.

COLOR DOS

The safest approach to hair color is to go to a salon and have a colorist do the job for you. If you're feeling naughty and want to do something dangerous at home, just be smart about it. Buy **rinse-out** color or a **color shampoo** that washes out. Or get some hair mascaras and have fun doodling. Don't do permanent color at home and expect to be happy with it.

Beach color: For a little accelerated summer lightening with the help of the sun, pack along a spray bottle filled with lemon juice mixed with water (for light hair color) or cranberry juice mixed with water (for dark hair). Spritz down your hair with your brew and comb through. When hair starts to dry, spritz it down again for more color.

COLOR DON'TS

Don't try these at home
Boiling Kool-Aid and pouring it on your hair: You'll have to live with orange hair until it grows out, because there's absolutely no way to get it out.

Spray-in lighteners: They'll turn hair orange.

HAIR BOREDOM... WHEN YOU FEEL LIKE YOU NEED A BIG CHANGE...

- **You've got really long hair**...you are bored with it and want a change. Cutting it all off is a big step, and you might be miserable. Instead, go a few inches shorter and see how you like it. Then, after a month or two, go a few more inches shorter. Ease into a short cut that you won't regret.

If you don't want to go shorter, but still want a little variety, try any of these:

Twist it back when it's wet so that hair dries with pretty texture.
Set it with rollers.
Iron it straight.
Crimp it.
Do two braids.
Do a high ponytail.
Do temporary color.
Go to a salon and ask for a blow-dry lesson so you can do it perfectly straight by yourself.

- **You've got medium-length hair**, it's not short and it's not long and you're not sure which way to go.

  Cut it short.

  Cut in bangs and let the rest grow long.

  Pull it back in a tight ponytail.

  Do hair mascara.

  Get highlights.

  Get a professional blow-dry.

  Try an up do that works for your hair like half up (the front) and the rest down.

  Do two side braids.

  Iron it.

  Do a set.

- **You've got really short hair**, you're bored and you can't cut any more off.

  Slick it back with gel.

Wear little clips or barrettes.

For a trendy, funky look, do really blond or really dark color just on the tips. (You can always cut it off later.)

PERMS

Don't even think about getting a perm (short for permanent wave) before you hit sixteen, since your hair texture may change as you get older. The truth is, I don't love perms at any age because they're designed to alter your hair's texture—something so basic and unique to you I think you should learn to love it!

My advice? Avoid perming. Try setting your hair with rollers instead—it gives the same look (probably without the frizziness), and you can always go back to your natural texture. (You can even do the set with perm rods to get the full effect.) A perm will **never wear off**. To get rid of it, you have to **grow it out**!

Body wave: It's still a perm and will have to be grown out or cut out to get rid of it. (The rod size is just bigger with a body wave.)

Home Perm:

IF SOMEONE OFFERS TO GIVE YOU A HOME PERM OR BODY WAVE, FIND ANY WAY YOU CAN TO REFUSE.

Leave immediately. Imagine that there are snakes in the room. Letting anyone (even someone who says she knows what she is doing) do a home perm on you is something you will **live to regret**!

MOST COMMON HAIR COMPLAINTS AND EASY SOLUTIONS

"My Hair Is Too Limp and Thin"

Use volumizing shampoo. Make sure it's clear, not creamy. Dilute it (see above) if you shampoo daily. Concentrate shampoo on scalp. Don't use conditioner. Use a detangler in the shower instead. Rinse hair really really well (three to four minutes) to get out any styling product goo.

When drying, hang head to the floor and flop hair over so that you dry roots in the opposite direction to which hair normally falls. Result? More volume.

"My Hair Is Dry and Brittle"

Do a weekly hair treatment. Work sesame oil (or leave-in conditioner) into wet hair and wrap head with a plastic bag. Leave in for 30 minutes. Rinse out. (Don't shampoo out.)

Also, look for alcohol-free styling products. Ones containing alcohol contribute to the dry, brittle state of your hair.

"I Hate My Flyaway Hair"

Buy static guard (the stuff you'd use on your clothes) and spray on your brush before using. Wash your brushes regularly because the hair left in your brush can pass static along to the hair still in your head.

Anti flyaway trick:

Spray a little nonaerosol hairspray into your hands and smooth hands down over hair working from the roots to ends. Don't use very much. Or, rub a spot of hand cream into palms of hands and gently pat on hair.

"Yuck, I Hate the Frizzies"

Spray your hair down with water. Work a drop of brilliance cream (one that adds shine) or leave-in conditioner into your hair. **Then don't touch your hair** (fingering it causes frizzies). Let it air dry.

BAD HAIR DAYS

We all have them. And, yes, there is something you can do. First don't panic.

If your hair is **long enough**, brush it really well (like I do—brush strokes distribute your hair's natural oils) and then pull it back in a ponytail or a braid.

If hair is **short**, gel it back. Don't pile on a million products. That will just weigh your hair down and make it feel dirty.

If all else fails, wear a baseball cap. (That's how I get out of the house!) Or, wear a bandanna or look around for some good hair accessories for your bad hair days.

Check out other hair help on www.salonaks.com. Read magazines and tear out your favorite hairstyles.

27 BACKSTAGE WITH BOBBI
COOL RUNWAY SECRETS

Doing makeup for the fashion shows is a totally high-pressure job. Sometimes the girls arrive late (like just before they are expected to put on their first looks), so I have only minutes to take off the makeup of whatever show they've done before and put on the look for the show we're doing. Of course, I have assistants. But there are girls who will only let me touch their faces—and I wouldn't have it any other way.

The things I've learned backstage translate perfectly well into everyday life. But it took the stressful experience backstage for me to come up with most of these tricks of my trade.

BACKSTAGE BASICS

1. Know your light. As a runway makeup artist, I've learned to be a master of lighting. If you do the wrong makeup for the light you will be in, it may "read" in a totally wrong way. Choose makeup that's correct for the lighting you will be in.

2. Mix it up. Blend three lip colors together for a custom color. Mix different lip colors and textures (matte with shimmer, for example). (Makeup artists never just use what you find in a single tube! That's why we're called artists!)

3. Blend your own foundation with moisturizer for a light tinted moisturizer.

4. Use yellow-tone foundation for the most natural look.

5. Soft pastel blush = Instant pretty.

6. Light shimmery colors brighten eyelids in harsh runway lighting.

7. Break the rules—who says you can't put lipstick on your cheeks as a creamy blush? Or, that you can't wear bronzer on your lips?

Vaseline Variations

Mix Vaseline with bronzer for one-toned face look—spread on eyelids, cheeks, forehead, and nose.

Put Vaseline on lips, then draw in all-over color with lip pencil.

Use Vaseline to condition and darken your eyebrows. (Be careful to avoid getting it in your eyes, though.)

Use it for dry heels, elbows, and cuticles.

Fast Fixers

Too heavy or pasty foundation?
- Put some moisturizer on your palms and gently press palms on face to tone down.

Too much blush?

- Blend away excess with a cotton powder puff.

Oil breakthrough?
- Blot gently with a powder puff dusted with powder.

Too-dark lip color?
- Layer on pale pink or white to lighten.

Too-bright lip color?
- Layer on beige (or foundation) to mute color.

Quick Cleanups

Oil-free makeup remover on a Q-Tip will lift mascara that's wandered off your lashes.

Oil-free remover will also soak up makeup on clothes. Use a paper towel instead of a tissue that will leave lint.

Oil-free makeup remover is the fastest all-around way to take a full face of makeup off and start over from ground zero. (Or, call it quits and go to bed!)

SMUDGING IT (in front of four Million Viewers)

Once when I was doing a demonstration on eye makeup on the *Today* show with Katie Couric, the model blinked as I was applying mascara and it smudged. I was instantly panicked since we were live and the cameras were really tight on the model's eye.

Just as I convinced myself that no one would see it, we were live on air and Katie said: "Oh Bobbi, even you smudge!" I seized the moment and said: "But Katie. It's good that I smudge, because it happens to everyone and now I can show you how to fix it."

I picked up a Q-Tip, dipped it into non-oily makeup remover, and it came right off. Pheeew!

28 THE ATHLETIC LOOK

BEING AN ATHLETE DOESN'T MEAN LOOKING LIKE A GUY.

So…you're a jock. That's cool, and should be a cool part of who you are. But being athletic shouldn't exclude caring about your looks. Most athletes do like girly stuff, too. Wearing mascara isn't a sign that you're not dedicated to your sport!

If you can reconcile the two (being athletic and being natural and pretty), the combination couldn't be more amazing. Thanks to your sports training and the athletic body it's given you, clothes look great on you. And thanks to your all-around muscle tone, you probably carry yourself tall and gracefully. All you need in the beauty department is a few fast grooming ideas and makeup tips. Then you'll look amazing.

NO MAKEUP IS OKAY, TOO!

EASY, NATURAL SPORT FACE— THE "MOST MINIMUM" EVERYDAY MAKEUP FOR JOCKS

Concealer

Tinted Moisturizer, SPF 15

Cream or Gel Blush

Natural Lip Color (it should match the color of your lips) or tinted lip balm, SPF 15

Brown mascara

Pre-game grooming: Step by step

1. Apply waterproof sunscreen (focus on nose, shoulders, knees—spots where the sun loves to burn) if you'll be playing outside. Otherwise, put a lightweight moisturizer on your face and body.

2. Put hair neatly back. If hair is long—do braids or a tight ponytail. If short—secure with barrettes any pieces that may fly into your face and distract you. Headbands are an option for any length hair.

3. Coat lips with SPF 15 lip balm (if game is outside) or a bit of gloss.

GYM BAG: GO-GIRL BASICS

- Lip balm (SPF 15)
- Sunscreen (Waterproof, SPF 15 or higher)
- Wide-Tooth Comb (Don't use a brush on wet hair!)
- Gentle, Everyday Shampoo (since washing hair daily with detergent shampoo is drying) Otherwise dilute the gym's shampoo.
- Detangler (for oily hair) or Conditioner (for dry hair)
- Body moisturizer or oil (apply just out of shower when skin is still wet)
- Scent (carry along a sample vial if you're going out afterward)

After Sports Makeup

Cool-Down: Don't apply makeup right after your workout, or you'll sweat it off. Wait until your body cools down completely (ten to fifteen minutes).

Sport Skin Care

- Carry along cleanser towelettes for your workout if you have oily skin or struggle with clogged pores (great for when there's no shower handy).
- Wash face after sweating (remember to bring face cleanser or soap into shower).
- Toner is good. Bring along cotton pads, too.
- Apply oil-free moisturizer while skin is still wet.

Sweat-Proof Makeup for Sports

There are times when athletes do wear makeup. Think about figure skaters, synchronized swimmers, and gymnasts. What these girls wear on their faces must stick in all possible situations. The key to sweat-proofing your makeup is knowing what to wear **and** what to skip:

1. Start with oil-control lotion.

2. Skip all-over foundation. Instead, use foundation to cover spots. Then "set" with powder and puff.

3. Use a waterproof eye pencil to smudge a line above lashes.

4. Use a waterproof lipstick or lip pencil all over with lip balm over top.

5. Skip blush—you'll get your own natural glow!

WINNING GOOD LOOKS:
THE BEST SPORTS STYLES

Serena & Venus Williams:

There is nothing more awesome than a sculpted athletic body. It shows strength and confidence and, to me, that is beautiful. Both Williams sisters have gorgeous cut bodies (that they are not afraid to show off in cut-out tennis dresses yes!). They broke new ground in the tennis world with their hair: beaded all over in braids. It's a good new look that's totally practical for tennis.

Despite all their similarities, they have their own looks and personalities. Venus, at six feet one inch, is the taller of the two, and somehow more intimidating across the net. Serena is more buff, like a sprinter. When the two team up to play doubles, they have it all! And, to top it off, they are great sports role models for young women everywhere. Their smiles are contagious.

Gabrielle Reece—Volleyball Player

She's a sports goddess—strong and muscular and gorgeous!

The World Champion U.S. Women's Soccer Team

Let's talk about the lasting impression the 1999 Women's Soccer Team made on the world! They were strong and tough, sweaty, gorgeous, and awesome. True champions. And incredible role models for girls everywhere. I think they look beautiful with no makeup—just sweat!

This is one of my treasured photos. Backstage at the Meadowlands in Rutherford, N.J., with my new friends Julie Foudy, Brandi Chastain, Mia Hamm, Carla Overbeck (and the rest of my sons and friends).

And that final moment when Brandi Chastain ripped off her jersey to reveal her (**Oh my god!**) rock-solid abs? That's the body we all should aspire to....And why not? We can all manage to make ourselves strong. With hard work, you'll see a great reward. It's all about strength and confidence. These women were sending a message loud and clear: **you** can do it! (I just met Brandi and teammate Julie Foudy and they're just as amazing in person as they seemed on television!)

"When I was a teenager, I had really short hair. Sometimes, after soccer practice, when I was in my sweats, people would think I was a boy. As a result, I had this constant fear of being called "young man" or "sir." To avoid that at all cost I would wear these ridiculously huge hoop earrings so that my gender was obvious. I look back at pictures and laugh at the earring concoctions I would come up with, just to say, "hey, I am a girl with short hair, not a guy!" I really believe that no matter how self-confident you are as a teenager, we all have our issues we deal with daily. The key is understanding that everyone has his or her issues, quirks and bouts of self-doubt. It is part of puberty! The comfort for teenagers should come in realizing that just like bad acne, these issues too shall pass. Now, go out

*there and put on those **huge** hoop earrings and laugh at yourself...the two keys to ensure happiness!"* **Julie Fowdy**

BOBBI'S OTHER ALL-TIME FAVORITE FEMALE ATHLETES:

Skier Picabo Street—I love her freckles!!! And her braid and laid-back beauty style.

Summer Sanders—Her freshness and lean muscles are great. It's awesome to watch the toned body of a swimmer.

Tennis Player Lindsay Davenport—She's so strong and uses her height (six feet two inches) to great advantage. I've loved watching her become more and more confident with her style.

GIRLS AND SPORTS: WHAT'S YOUR FIT?

Get moving! It feels great to exercise. Nothing in life gives us a more instant sense of well-being and confidence. Exercise makes you look better instantly, too. You'll have a flushed happy glow after working out. I was a latecomer to exercise (I started at twenty), and I'll always regret that I didn't do something earlier. In my teen years, I didn't have the confidence or the endurance to play sports.

But when I was growing, girls didn't have the option of doing sports. Organized female sports teams basically didn't really exist. (Title 9, passed in 1979, changed all that by requiring schools to offer equal opportunity in sports to boys and girls.) In my day, ballet was the only activity option, and, believe me, I was not put on this earth to do pirouettes. I took it anyway since everyone else was. My teacher either ignored me or told me how bad I was. So it wasn't long before I dropped out to do drama classes and piano. (My piano career wasn't so much better.)

Today is a different story. On Saturday mornings, I see little girls arriving with their fathers at a field near my house to play soccer. It's awesome to witness the confidence these girls possess. They know it is not about being the best or better than the rest, but about being their own personal best and about being a team player. They get huge rewards just by putting out their best effort.

Soccer has a position for almost every energy level. If you're hyper, you play forward. If you're bigger and tougher, play backfield. If you're not a runner but are strategic and can handle pressure, try playing goalie. Basketball, softball, volleyball, and field hockey are sports that offer similar challenges to girls.

But if team sports aren't your thing, consider an individual sport, like swimming, or track and field. You still get the thrill of belonging but the competition is more personal (and usually intense).

If you are more of an independent thinker, consider taking up one or more of the following activities:

Ballet I flunked out, but I really admire the girls who stick with it! Ballet builds strong postural muscles and discipline. *Eating Disorder Alert* Serious dancers get serious about having the "right" ballet body—very thin and delicate with long muscles. Those who don't have this look naturally often starve themselves skinny. It's not worth it. (*See page 75 for more information.*)

Gymnastics A good activity to start when you're young that helps build strong bodies and great athleticism. You can take gymnastics classes just for fun or get competitive and superinvolved. (*See eating disorder alert, above.*)

Yoga Great for chilling and toning. Don't go expecting just a blow-off workout, though. Depending on the type of yoga, it can be aerobic and pretty intense.

Disco Dancing to music you love is fun and a good workout. I have to admit that the disco beat always gets me going.

Walking Wear headphones and start slowly at first, going short distances. You can start out with a ten-minute workout and build up to an hour. Try speed walking up and down hills. There's a good chance your walking will turn into jogging, but either one is a great workout.

Tap How much fun is this? Take a tap class with a friend for a good workout and a few laughs. Other dance options: aerobic dance, African jazz-funk, modern, ballroom.

Jumping rope Not just a playground toy, the jump rope can provide a serious workout. Start working up to a hundred consecutive jumps and work on "boxer's" form, keeping your feet close to the ground.

Kick Boxing A blast. And a great way to blow off steam.

Ice Skating, in-line skating, roller skating These activities are all great for your legs and butt. And a lot of fun. Just be smart when you skate around town: Wear a helmet and pads.

Biking Whether it's transportation to school or an off-road ride after hours, biking is great exercise. To increase your workout, do drills on hills one day and then go for distance the next. And remember, it's stupid not to wear a helmet despite what it does to your hair. Spinning classes to music are a great indoor sweat-it-out option.

Basic P.E. Class Workout push-ups, sit-ups, and a two-mile jog. It feels like work (and it is!) but it works wonders on your body.

The Montclair Traveling Soccer Team
I see these guys practicing all the time and I'm inspired by their energy and team spirit. They happen to be great athletes, as well. We spent some time together one Saturday morning just after their practice.

Here they are just after practice. The truth is they looked fabulous.

I did light makeup: sheer lip gloss and tawny blush. Okay, I admit it…I did cover up one zit. Natural sports makeup like I did on these girls is my all-time favorite.

Go crazy! Who says jocks can't wear makeup? I brought along a bag of wild lipstick colors and let everyone choose the color they wanted to wear. The result? Wow lips in bright orange, deep purple, red, dark brown. (I also added a little blush to balance the strong mouth.) Only one girl hated her choice and went back for seconds.

Me and my great friend Chloe!
Following spread: Soccer Team—Clean, perfect faces. And the girls with fun lipsticks! Awesome!

29 MOTHER-DAUGHTER BEAUTY

Jen Araki is a model we booked to demonstrate makeup for this book. When she arrived at the studio with her mother, we all saw the same thing. Two generations of great natural beauty style. The best part? They really like each other and had traveled together to New York so that Jen could live out her modeling fantasy. So far, so good.

"My mom tells me that I don't need a lot of makeup." —Bridgette

"My mother tells me I should always wear makeup." —Janaina

"My mom tells me that I look like my uncle Doug and that my eyes are too far apart." —Kimberly

"My mom tells me that I'm talented." —Jessica

"My mom tells me I can do anything if I try." —Becky

"My mom tells me I am spacy." —Sarah

"My mom tells me that I am pretty and that I look like she did when she was younger." —Carlyle

"My mother tells me that I am too critical of myself." —Julie

Jen and her mom (clearly they share the same beauty gene pool). Two true beauties.

"My mother tells me that I have an attitude problem."
—Andrea

When I was a little girl, I felt that there was no one as glamorous as my mother. I used to sit on the floor and look up as she artfully applied her make-up. Her skin was perfect (she was a really young mother). She always started with a face cream. Then it was her eyes and eyebrows. She used real charcoal artist pencils to sketch in her perfectly arched brows. She applied a very matte white shadow as a base for her eyelids. (Looking back now, I realize how heavy and overdone it must have seemed!) Then she wet a thin brush to apply '60s-style liquid eyeliner on her top lid only and continued the line outside the eye area and finished to a point.

I remember watching my mom putting on her sexy black false lashes. She wet individual lashes with glue and used a toothpick to put them on. My favorite thing that she would do (and still my favorite move—something I do all the time) is to rub a bronzing stick high on the cheeks for a healthy glow. She'd then reach for her pale whitish pink lipstick and apply it right out of the tube. It always amazed me that her lipsticks retained their slanted-top shapes. (She still does this, by the way!)

And what did my mom wear during this procedure? Stockings, bra, panties, and high spiked heels. Maybe this image explains my tendency to wear jeans, flat shoes, and ponytails all the time.

Best of Buddies

Top: Bobbi and her Nana. Left: Aunt Alice. Right: Bobbi and her mom.

MY OTHER BEAUTY ROLE MODELS

My Grandmother (my "nana")—I remember my "nana" taking her lipstick and rubbing it on her lined cheeks and then, afterward to her lips. She never wore foundation, eye shadow, or mascara. But tons of rose oil. I definitely identify more with my nana's beauty style than I do with my own mother's...maybe beauty style skips generations.

My Aunt Alice—She would always show up in simple but unexpected colors—like lilac eye shadow with white lipstick. She still wears these colors and I've even made the shades she loves most for my own company.

My First Makeup Kit: It was a shoebox filled with discarded makeup. And since it was my mother who gave me this kit, it contained lots of white eye shadow, charcoal pencils, and too-pink lipstick. Oh yeah...and lots of white frosty nail polish. It didn't take me long to outgrow this kind of makeup!

WHAT I LEARNED FROM MY MOM

A lot...My mom was very generous and loved to teach me just the way her mom did with her. I learned that:

1. Sleep and rest and happiness are the backbones of beauty.

2. Healthy foods go a long way in upping your beauty quotient.

3. It's a bad idea to go to bed without washing your face and applying cream. (There's no excuse if you are exhausted—just keep a few facial wipes around. You'll regret it in the morning if you don't make the effort before you crash.)

4. Good grooming (i.e., regular haircuts, clean hair) makes a huge difference in terms of your self-image.

5. Organize your cosmetics and keep only what you really use. Find dividers or the perfect fishing tackle box for your makeup so you can put your finger on what you need fast.

6. Love yourself for who you are—each of us is special and we're most likely to be happiest when we believe it!

TEACHING YOUR MOM
THE MAKEUNDER LESSON

There are definitely lots of lessons you can teach your mother about makeup, too. Probably the most important thing you have to tell her is to relax with and be more casual about her makeup. If you take a gentle, helpful approach, hopefully she'll be open to what you've got to say!

• If she tends to wear the same lip color all the time, try to get her into gloss. Tell her that gloss is sexy and more relaxed!

• If she seems to wear the same amount of make-up all the time, talk her into volume control—wearing less sometimes (like for day or on vacations) and wearing obviously more other times (like for a party). Wearing the exact same face every day makes her a slave to makeup.

• If your mom's hairstyle has been the same as long as you can remember, encourage her to find an update. Help her book an appointment for a consultation and offer to go with her. Be sure she goes to the best salon in your city. My point of view? A good haircut should be able to look good air-dried with no styling time.

• Try to get your mother to do something young (it's sure to make her feel young!), like wearing barrettes in her hair, trying a strange nail polish color, wearing a fun, shimmery shadow. Tell her that she's sure to thank you for it later.

MOTHER-DAUGHTER SPA NIGHT

A fun evening for me as a teenager was a stay-at-home beauty night. My mother and I would put masks on our faces. (I loved the peel-off kind.) We'd soak our hands in a soapy bowl filled with water for our manicures. (My mother warned me never to cut my cuticles and unfortunately I do…once you start, you have to do it often!) We'd plunk our feet in a sudsy soup pot. We'd wet pumice stones to rub the rough spots on our heels. If we were ambitious we'd put deep conditioner in our hair, wrap our heads in Saran Wrap, and then sit under one of those old-fash-

ioned dryers. When we were done, we each had a big bowl of ice cream. (I'm sure it was low fat—my mother was the original health nut!) You and your mom can work up your own treatments or try some of my basics. Or, if your mother plans to visit a spa, ask her to re-create the experience at home with you!

Mother (Sometimes) Knows Best

Watch your mother because there are a lot of things you can learn from her. The lessons you will take from her are invaluable and will stay with you forever. If you are rolling your eyes thinking, "But you haven't ever met *my* mom—she has nothing to teach me!" I probably have (or someone a lot like your mom) and I stand by my statement: You'll be grateful for what you learn from her.

Dark Circles: They are hereditary. Watch how your mom covers hers, she probably knows best.

Nails: Do your nails when your mom does to pick up her tried-and-true pointers.

Hair: If your hair is anything like your mom's, chances are she has learned how to best deal with it…i.e., the right hairstyle, color, cut, etc.

MESSAGE TO MOMS

Please remember that it is hard today to be a teenager. Body image, competition, etc. Be deliberate in your efforts to be a positive role model.

1. Do anything in your powers to give your daughter confidence and to help her feel at ease with her looks.

2. **Remember**: Don't force what you don't like about yourself onto your daughter. Don't tell her that her nose is too big if you don't like your own nose. Don't comment on her weight if it doesn't otherwise bother her.

3. Accentuate the positive. Compliment her on her beautiful hair, skin, lips, etc.

4. Let your daughter be herself…encourage her to express herself…and to **experiment**!

5. Give your daughter the makeup basics and then allow her to play. She'll eventually come to a look that's best for her.

6. Control only what you can control. Ultimately you will not be able to stop your daughter if she wants to dye her hair purple or to pluck out all her eyebrows. If you keep your channels of communications open, you can have a greater influence over her decisions. Don't be a dictator.

7. **The most important thing!**
Try to keep love and respect alive in your relationship. Remember: Your daughter is a member of a new generation and she has to do what's best for her. A girl's gotta do what a girl's gotta do! And she is not you!

MOTHERS AND MAKEUP: SOMETIMES YOU SHOULD LISTEN. SOMETIMES YOU SHOULDN'T.

TROUBLES WITH MOM

When is a girl old enough to do her own thing? I'm sick of my mom telling me I am not allowed to shave my legs or wear shadow.

It's normal to want to experiment. It's normal to want to sneak a little gloss or shadow on the bus on the way to school. My advice is to keep things looking natural so that you won't get caught. A little makeup is probably not worth getting grounded over.

How can a girl keep her relationship positive with her mom when every day there's a battle over what she can and cannot do?

- We all go through ups and downs in our relationships with our moms.
- Try to remind your mom that she was once your age. Ask her how she dealt with her own mom when she wanted to do something that seemed outrageous to granny.
- Sometimes mothers get their own identities wrapped up in their daughters'. Remind your mom (in as gentle and nonsarcastic way as possible) that she is **not you**!

How do you deal with a mom who says NO to everything: "No, you *can't* shave your legs." "No, you *can't* wear mascara." "No, you *can't* pierce your ears."

Try to be patient. Find the right moment (i.e., not when everyone is rushing out of the house in the morning) to sit down with your mom to discuss when she thinks it'd be okay to do what you want. Work out a plan together.

I didn't have things so perfectly figured out myself... I remember that I once went out and double-pierced my ears (against my mother's wishes). It was no surprise that I got grounded.

Left: Hanging out together, Halley and her mom. Right: Nico and her mom showing off their gorgeous smiles and their very different looks.

30 ROCK 'N' ROLL BABES: HIP BEAUTY STYLE

Rock'n' style hair that's tousled…a piece that falls into your face…nothing too perfect…showing your bra strap…lipstick put on fast and slightly lopsided…nothing is too perfect…it's fast (or looks that way), sometimes hard, and usually wild…sexy-tough glam is the message.

Getting a "**look**" is one of the most important things a performer must do. That's what will separate her from all the rest of the wannabe singers and make her stand apart and shine! A performer's look is about the mood she wants to create. Singers also have to continually re-create themselves, sending out a new image with each new album. That way every time her new CD hits the stores she comes across fresh. Evolution is essential. Here's the beauty scoop on a group of stars who've mastered the art of evolution and represent the best in rock 'n' roll beauty babes:

Blaque

These girls' style is fun and funky, very girly, and experimental. They all do different hair and makeup that reflects their own personal style, best they work really well together and are truly kind and nice.

Britney Spears

She's pretty and wholesome. She wears the right colors for a blond. She does a smokey eye with lighter color on top. Her skin is dewey and flawless.

She has an incredibly pretty look.

Aaliyah

She's got what most of us want: model beauty but her own unique style.

Jewel

She goes from simple and outdoorsy to sophisticated and classic. She looks amazing with dark glossy lips and dark lined eyes. Jewel always comes across as classy, never harsh or trashy. And her skin is extraordinary.

Courtney Love

Another genius at transformation, Courtney Love has gone from trashy to glam to minimal and back again. Still, I think her softer look is the most beautiful.

Madonna

She started it all and is the original chameleon. My favorite look of all of her various incarnations is blond, soft, and natural.

LeAnne Rimes

She has a sweet normal kind of pretty that's totally approachable. Leanne has a soft look with a strong brow which is a great combination.

Sheryl Crow

The coolest woman on the planet. I love that I've had the chance to do her makeup. Sheryl has an amazing body and her short hair sets her apart and suits her beautifully.

BOBBI ENDSPEAK

NOW THAT I'VE TOLD YOU EVERYTHING YOU'LL EVER NEED TO KNOW ABOUT YOUR LOOKS, I WANT YOU TO PROMISE NOT TO TAKE ANY OF IT TOO SERIOUSLY!!!

You've heard the expression: Beauty is only skin deep. Nothing could be closer to the truth. Yet it is my hope that by feeling confident with your physical looks, you'll develop the inner self-assurance to do whatever it is you're most driven to achieve. Be a drummer in a rock band. Be the top of your class. Be fluent in French. Be the top tennis player in your state. Be a great friend, daughter, sister, granddaughter. Be worthy. Be involved. Be connected. Feel the ability to do anything. I will have accomplished a great deal if this book gives you the confidence to so something meaningful. If you are temporarily stuck over what that is, I've started a list for you....

Ten Things to Do if You Find Yourself Crazy-Obsessing Over Your Looks**

1. Volunteer to hold the babies at a children's hospital or the intensive care unit of a general hospital. For them, touching is healing.

2. Get involved in a team sport.

3. If you love animals, investigate how to help increase adoptions at your local ASPCA. Or become a dog walker.

4. Read to kids. Volunteer to be a big sister/tutor for a grade-school kid who needs help.

5. Do yoga. Learn to meditate. Run.

6. Visit an elderly neighbor. Arrange to visit a friend or relative in his or her retirement community.

7. Organize the clean-up of a park or roadway.

8. Make an effort to include someone new to your school in activities and conversations. Invite her to a party with you. Be friendly.

9. Get all your friends together for a closet sale—selling things that they make or their own clothes that they've never worn or have grown tired of. Give the money to a cause you like.

10. Get better perspective of your life from a distance…go away—to French camp, sailing, computer, or riding camp. Or, go on a teen tour of someplace fun or exotic. Or get a summer job as an au pair somewhere far away.

**If you are truly unhappy, find someone you can confide in—i.e., a teacher, parent, friend, or doctor or a psychologist/psychiatrist. There is no reason to feel despair. Talking about your problems is the first step toward solving them.

PRETTY ON THE INSIDE = PRETTY ON THE OUTSIDE

INDEX OF RESOURCES

I. SHOP TALK
The places to find the best of everything

I find the coolest things in the oddest places, which is what makes beauty shopping so much fun. Thank goodness there's no such thing as one-stop shopping for beauty supplies.

Art Supply Stores
For high-quality brushes that aren't that expensive. You can sometimes find cool boxes for supplies, as well.

Beauty Supply Stores
Alcone is a favorite because it's convenient for me and carries things from all over the world. Check out its Lucite lip color and foundation palettes (by Krylon) and makeup artist cases. Located in New York City (tel: 212-633-0551); Alcone does mail order and also offers classes.

Health Food Stores
Here I love to find natural toothpaste, deodorant (Tom's of Maine makes one I like), creams, and sunblock. I can always find Burt's Beeswax lip balm.

You can find really nice essential oils here to use on really dry skin, for massage, or to smooth down really curly hair.

Department Stores

Think investment beauty…If you are going to spend the money on department store products, be sure you take advantage of the service available to you. That means you should find a sales associate who you can relate to and connect with. You should also like the makeup and general style of the sales associate. (The lady wearing thick pancake makeup and tons of hairspray probably won't be the one who relates best to you.)

The best things to buy here?

- Your perfect concealer or tinted moisturizer (ask for help in finding the right color).
- Your perfect skin-care plan. Again, ask for help—don't feel committed to buy anything unless you are certain you've got the right thing for you.
- Avoid buying impulse items like lipstick or gloss or wild colors that you'll grow bored with and toss out in a few weeks.

Drugstores

For fun lip and nail colors, glitter eye makeup as well as your bathroom basics: body lotion, shampoo, conditioner, sponges, Q-Tips, etc.

Ricky's

This is a New York City secret. Ricky's is a dive of a drugstore, but when you start looking closely you'll find amazing tools and products from all over. Mail order is available. The best part? This beauty addict's heaven stays open until midnight! Soho location is 590 Broadway between Houston and Prince (tel: 212-226-5552).

Websites

There's a new beauty website every day. Here are a few of the basics.

www.bobbibrown.com

www.ibeauty.com

www.beauty.com

www.gloss.com

www.indulge.com

Catalogs

The Bliss spa in Manhattan is a groovy beauty mecca. Its catalog, *BlissOut,* is fun to read even if you never plan to splurge at the spa! (To order, call: 888-243-8825.)

II. ACNE ADVICE: GOING TO THE DERMATOLOGIST

Dr. Ellen Genler, a leading Manhattan dermatologist, sets us straight on what a teen can expect on a visit to a skin doctor.

The Chat…The Exam

1. Be prepared to discuss your cleansing/moisturizing routine. (It'd be smart to bring along any zit medication you currently use.) The dermatologist will want to work with you to find something that's not too drying.

2. The doctor will probably talk to you about makeup. (Again, it's smart to bring along whatever you use.) He or she will be trying to cut down on any products that could be irritating or that you could be allergic to.

3. The doctor will look at your skin through a magnifying mirror.

The Treatment

There is help for everyone—it just depends on how serious your acne is.

For occasional breakouts or blackheads: A doctor would prescribe a topical (a cream or gel) antibiotic. Ask for specific instructions (i.e., whether you should use a moisturizer in addition to the medication).
When you'll see results: four weeks.

For acne (including inflamed pimples): Your dermatologist will prescribe an antibiotic that you take in pill form. Ask for specific instructions about foods you can eat (sometimes milk products must be avoided), whether your skin will be more sensitive to the sun, the time of day to take the pill, etc.
When you'll see results: one to two months.

For serious acne (inflamed pimples that will lead to scarring): Your doctor may talk to you about going on Acutane, an intense antibiotic. (Since Acutane causes birth defects, your doctor will want to discuss whether you have a sex life and, if so, what form of birth control you use.) Acutane can change your life, however. Even if nothing else works, results are amazing.
When you'll see results: six weeks to two months.

Facial Facts

Dr. Genler doesn't usually advise facials for her teen patients because she finds that the massage and manipulation can actually irritate the skin. It's just not worth it. When facials could be useful? In the case of a million blackheads when the facialist really focuses on clearing them out.

ONE INFLAMED ZIT

Don't touch it!!!! Call your dermatologist to arrange for a quick emergency visit (a drive-by session). The doctor will either inject the pimple with cortizone (zap and it's gone) or lance it to drain the pus.

Doctor's Warning: By attempting to do surgery on your own face, you risk creating open sores that'll take a lot longer to heal and could result in scars.

III. GETTING REAL ABOUT WEIGHT LOSS

One Medical Expert's Advice

What works for me might not necessarily work for every girl reading this book. That's why I consulted Ronald A. Ruden, M.D., a Manhattan physician who specializes in nutrition and metabolic disorders. Here's his message for girls fighting a weight issue.

THE BIG PICTURE: Try to make the best of what you've got. I don't expect a chunky teenager with zits to wake up and say, "Boy, do I look great!"

WHAT'S HAPPENING IN YOUR BODY:

Adolesence is an extremely stressful time for girls in terms of their body image and approach to food.

The female homones act as a stresser on the brain and it takes until the end of adolescence for the brain to get used to these hormones. (These hormones are like a hot tub for the brain. It feels unbearably hot at the beginning but, over time, you get used to it.) Essentially, you don't feel under control.

Hormones drive a behavior that is counterproductive to looking your best. And you must take steps to help avoid letting that behavior become destructive to your happiness. In early adolescence, that means craving food, sometimes sweets, and sometimes greasy junk food.

LOSING WEIGHT TAKES EFFORT, EFFORT, EFFORT

Nothing you want to do that goes against the biological forces in your body (i.e., those stupid **hormones**!) is going to be easy.

This is your problem. It's not your mother's problem. It's not your father's problem…you are responsible for your actions and your actions have consequences.

THE GENES YOU WERE DEALT: Everybody has a different genetic inheritance. If your parents are heavy, it is more than likely that you will be heavy. Some kids will find that they will gain weight by eating very little, while their best friends don't gain an ounce eating boxes of doughnuts all the time. If you let this unfairness upset you, you will never be happy with the gains you personally make.

Accept what your genetics has given you. This is no reason to be angry or upset.

THERE IS NO MIRACLE DIET

The key to learning how to eat and maintain a body weight is to create your own diet: No one diet works for everybody. Don't waste your money on the latest trendy diet.

Besides, going from diet to diet to diet won't solve your problem. If weight is really an issue (i.e., you're seriously overweight and can't get a handle on it), go to a pediatric nutritionist (since this can be costly—a consultation runs around $150—be sure to include your parents in your thinking). The nutritionist will outline a plan and program specially for you so that (with work, work, work) you can achieve your goals.

Many young people can't control their eating. Kids binge, especially when they're under stress. It seems as if they can't help themselves. Losing or controlling weight is a very hard thing to do. But it's not impossible. It works a little. Then there's sometimes failure. This turns into a cycle that can be extremely disappointing.

All you can do is try your best to achieve your goal. In persistence lies victory. Don't beat yourself up. Tomorrow is another day. Try again then.

Kids start associating the struggle with failure. They feel that what they're doing won't ultimately work… you've got to find a system that'll work for you.

If you identify with all of the above, join the club: **you are not alone**.

THE MOMENT WE'RE LIVING

One hundred years ago being skinny was considered ugly. A tan was considered ugly. A big meaty frame with pale skin was **the look**.

ACTION PLAN

Below are the four areas to think about…sort of a checklist of things to do in terms of taking control of your calories. If you do all these things, you will be able to maximize what you can do with your body so that you feel good about yourself. We were not all born to be Kate Moss.

I. Calories count. (Learn the math!)

Get to know the calorie count of your favorite foods. How many calories in a slice of pizza? A Hershey's bar? Make a list of the forty to fifty things you eat most often.

Map up a couple of diets using your favorite foods that meet the caloric level you need to keep to make gradual change. The best way to start? Buy a little calorie book. You can often find them at the checkout at a supermarket.

Your weight (in kilograms) X .28 = the number of calories needed to maintain your weight.
To drop weight, drop fat in your diet by 10 percent to 20 percent and try to make up a diet based on those foods.

Note: Be sure to take a multivitamin and calcium supplements. Any girl trying to lose weight needs to ensure she's getting her basic nutrients.

Also be aware that when you eat and how much you eat both count. Starving yourself all day, then eating a huge dinner, isn't a good way to go.

If creating your own smart eating plan to lose weight doesn't work, you'll have to change what you eat.

One pound of fat = 3,500 calories

Next step: If you need 2,000 calories to maintain your body weight, you need to cut down 20 percent of calories (to 1,600) (check a pounds-to-calories conversion chart).

II. The type of food you eat matters.

This is a tricky concept: People respond differently to different foods. Some people lose weight on a low-carbohydrate diet while others gain. Most individuals know which foods make them gain weight.

If, after you formulate your diet you are not seeing results, it's time to change the type of foods you eat:

Plan A

Decrease the carbs—and increase your protein.
Cut back on sweets, bread, rice, and pasta. Increase fresh fruits and vegetables and proteins. Try that for two months using the same caloric amounts.

Plan B

If that doesn't work, try a diet that's higher in carbo-hydrates (eat whole grain bread, brown rice, pasta) and low in fat, and you might see better results.

Each person is an individual. But one-size-fits-all diet books continue to sell.

III. What you eat and when you eat it matters.

Again, everyone is different. If by eating three meals a day (breakfast, lunch, and dinner), you are unable to lose weight, try eating a larger number of meals. Before you do backflips, know that each of, say, six meals (breakfast, morning snack, lunch, afternoon snack, dinner, evening snack) should be kept to a smaller portion. Some people do very well with that.

Other people find that if they eat carbohydrates in the morning and less in the afternoon and evening it helps them lose weight. Or, vice versa. Think about the timing of food. A large meal at nighttime could sabotage your efforts.

The absolutely wrong biological thing to do? Starve yourself.

By not eating you slow down your metabolism. Anything you do eat will not be as readily metabo-lized. Keep your metabolism going by eating throughout the day (and exercising, see below).

IV. Exercise counts.

Think of your body as a machine. You need to run the machine longer, faster, and harder to burn more fuel or calories. Exercise is also your insurance policy. You'll be better able to keep weight off if you exercise.

In order to sustain any hard-won weight loss, exercise is critical.

Doing a small amount of exercise every day is the best approach. Try to burn 200 calories daily by walking, jogging, swimming—whatever. **Do something you like and then stick with it!** See it in terms of calories, not exercise. Set out to burn 200 calories in a day.

If you struggle with severe obesity, see a professional. There may be biological stuff going on that only a doctor can figure out.

NOTE TO PARENTS: Being overweight is your child's problem. You should ask her if it bothers her. If it does, try to find a way to solve it together. (Screaming at her that she'll never be loved or will never find happiness won't be productive.) You should be supportive…not directive. DON'T BE CRITICAL. Your daughter needs to solve the problem herself. REMEMBER: This is the age when kids don't listen to their parents. Pushing them into something is exactly the biologically wrong thing to do, and your efforts will be doomed to failure. Don't lose sight of the fact that you really do want to help her.

ACKNOWLEDGMENTS

Bobbi and Annemarie would like to thank Diane Reverand and Patricia van der Leun for their energy, encouragement, and commitment to this project. Matthew Guma for his keeping everything together. Troy Word for his amazing photos. And Sam Shahid and Carlos Frederico Meira Farina for their vision, creativity, and insistance.

We are deeply grateful to the following teenage girls who gave so generously of their time for this project and who shared with us their most personal joys and fears:

Caitlin Aloise, Nefertiti Alves, Sara Armour, Janaina Aufiero, Bridgette Berra, Gretchen Berra, Lindsay Berra, Beverly Bolton, Chloe Carden, Sarah Carden, Amy Chaplin, Sara Covey, Amanda Davenport, Jessica Drewitz, Carey Felgendreger, Nikki Fitzmaurice, Jessica Foster, Michelle Foster, Julie Garrison, Maggie Goudsmit, Lauren Held, Rebecca Hessel, Tia Holland, Chloe Katz, Lisa Kress, Alexis O. Kier, Korina, Arielle Korwin, Jackie Krupa, Alex La Mantia, Katlin Leo, Mallory Leo, Hayley Lubarsky, Julia Norton, Raven Magrath, Robin Magrath, Jaime Mass, Sabrina Messina, Alex Mullins, Julie Minsky, Becky Moore, Ellen Munn, Lara Pinto, Rebecca Plofker, Sarah Porter, Melissa Rassas, Alyse Richards, Reia Robbins, Haley Rothman, Devon Roy, Taylor Roy, Nicole Salamone, Alyssa Samson, Carlyle Sargeant, Saskia, Lisa Seiffert, Jessica Shaw, Chloe Silber, Amanda Silver, Emily Silver, Adrienne Thal, Andrea Toth, Jillian Treadwell, Julia Maria Vasquez, Katie Vernon, Laura Warshauer, Nina Whitley, Rachel Wilkin, Kia Williams.

We would also like to recognize the contribution of the following friends:

Jessica Aufiero, Julie Berman, Rochelle Bloom, Rick Burda, Amy Burrous, Elite Model Management, Randy Farell-Forstein of AKS Salon, Ed Gold, Dennis Golonka, Rebecca Greenfield, Ron Hill, Alex Huara of AKS Salon, Industria Superstudios, IMG Models, Kris Johnson, Harry Josh, Leah Karp, Carolyn Kramer, Hollie Levy, Annette Lian-Williams, Rachel Low, Beth Mann, Suzanne Mendelsohn, Milk Studios, Next New Faces, Ann Nolte & Jeff Mahshie of Chaiken, PR Consulting, Daniel Petrull of AKS Salon, Jean Marie Quinta, Ken Robinson, Maria Romano, Suzanna Romano of AKS Salon, Paul Rowland and Nancy Ortiz of Women Model Management, Amy Roy, John Turner, Sheila Rogers, Laura Shanahan, Brooke Shields, Ralph Vestbom, Jessica Weinstein, Marcus Williamson.

Bobbi wants to especially thank her mother Sandra who gave her all to teach me when I was a teenager. And to the amazing men in my life who fill me with love—Steven, Dylan, Dakota, Duke, and Joe (Dad).

9 10 8

First published in the United States in 2000 by HarperCollins Publishers Inc.

First Published in the United Kingdom in 2000 by Ebury Press
Random House
20 Vauxhall Bridge Road
London SW1V 2SA

Random House Australia (Pty) Limited
20 Alfred Street, Milsons Point, Sydney
New South Wales 2062, Australia

Random House New Zealand Limited
18 Poland Road, Glenfield
Auckland 10, New Zealand

Random House South Africa (Pty) Limited
Endulini, 5A Jubilee Road
Parktown 2193, South Africa

The Random House Group Limited Reg. No. 954009
www.randomhouse.co.uk

A CIP catalogue for this book is available from the British Library
ISBN 0 09 187817 9
ISBN13 978 0 09 187817 7

Designed by Shahid & Company

Printed and bound by Appl Druck, Wemding, Germany